Learning to Program in
Python >>

P.M. Heathcote

Published by
PG Online Limited
The Old Coach House
35 Main Road
Tolpuddle
Dorset
DT2 7EW
United Kingdom
sales@pgonline.co.uk
www.pgonline.co.uk
2017

PG ONLINE

Graphics: Paul Raudner / PG Online Ltd

Design and artwork: PG Online Ltd

First edition 2017

A catalogue entry for this book is available from the British Library

ISBN: 978-1-910523-11-7

Copyright © PM Heathcote, 2017

Printed on FSC certified paper
Printed by Bell and Bain Ltd, Glasgow, UK.

Preface

Programming is fun! Trial and error is to be encouraged and you should type all of the examples and try all the exercises to get used to entering and debugging programs and to see how the programs run.

Python is one of the most popular programming languages both in schools and in industry. Python is used by Google, NASA, Instagram, Facebook and thousands of other companies to develop their applications. It is easy to learn and is a suitable language for tackling projects from school onwards.

This book is intended for individuals and students who may have done some programming in other languages, but are not familiar with Python. It is intended that users of the book should work through the book sequentially, starting at Chapter 1. However, it will be a useful reference book for students on a programming course or anyone working on a programming project.

It teaches basic syntax and programming techniques, and introduces three built-in Python modules:

- **Tkinter**, used for building a graphical user interface, which is an option that some users may like to include in their project work.

- **SQLite**, which enables the creation and processing of a database from within a Python program. This provides an alternative to writing to a text file when data needs to be stored and retrieved.

- **pdb**, Python's debugging module, which can be used to help find elusive logic errors.

Questions and exercises are included throughout every chapter. Over 120 Python programs for all the examples and exercises given in the book may be downloaded from **www.pgonline.co.uk**. We strongly advise you to write your own code, and check your solutions against the sample programs provided.

Enjoy – the sky's the limit!

Downloading Python 3

Python is available to be downloaded free from https://www.python.org/downloads/. The version used in this book is version 3.6. All the programs have been written and tested in IDLE, Python's own integrated development environment. Many schools and individuals may prefer to use alternative development environments and the book is equally applicable to these.

Contents

Chapter 1
Data types, operators and I-O

Objectives

- Run commands in interactive mode
- Use string, numeric and Boolean data types and operators
- Learn the rules and guidelines for naming variables
- Use input and output statements

Programming in Python

Python is a popular, easy-to-learn programming language. A Python program is simply a series of instructions written according to the rules or **syntax** of the language, usually designed to perform some task or come up with a solution to a problem. You write the instructions, and then the computer translates these instructions into binary machine code which the computer can execute. It will do this using a translator program, which could be either a **compiler** or an **interpreter**. Python uses elements of both an interpreter and a compiler.

Python comes with an **integrated development environment** called **IDLE** which enables you to enter your program, save it, edit it, translate it to machine code and run it once it is free of syntax errors. If you have written a statement wrongly, that will be reported by the interpreter as a syntax error, and you can correct it and try again.

Programming in interactive mode

Python has two modes of entering and running programs. In **interactive mode**, you can type instructions and Python will respond immediately. This is very useful for trying out statements that you are not sure about, and is a good place to start. However, you cannot save a program that you have written in interactive mode. This has to be done in **script mode**, described in the next chapter.

1

To begin an interactive session, from the **Start** menu choose **Python 3.x /IDLE**. You will see a screen similar to the one below:

```
Python 3.6.0 Shell                                               —    □    ✕
File  Edit  Shell  Debug  Options  Window  Help
Python 3.6.0 (v3.6.0:41df79263a11, Dec 23 2016, 07:18:10) [MSC v.1900 32 bit (In
tel)] on win32
Type "copyright", "credits" or "license()" for more information.
>>> |
```

Python IDLE (interactive window)

In this window, which is called the Python Shell window, you can type commands at the prompt, >>>.

```
>>> print("Hello World")
```

The Python interpreter responds to your command and you will see Hello World appear on the next line, followed by a new line with the prompt.

Data types

String data type

In the above command, "Hello World" is a data type known as a **string**. A string is simply one or more characters enclosed in quote marks, and it doesn't matter whether you use single or double quotes. If your string contains speech or a quotation, you can use whichever type of quote mark you did not use to enclose the whole string:

```
>>> print("He said 'Hello!'")
He said 'Hello!'
```

The symbol + is used to **concatenate**, or join together, two or more strings.

```
>>> "John" + " " + "Riddell"
'John Riddell'
```

Note that numbers enclosed in quotes, or input as strings, behave as strings, not numbers.

```
>>> "7" + "3"
'73'
```

Numeric data types and operators

A number can be either **integer** (a whole number) or **floating point**, (a number with a decimal point) referred to in Python as **int** and **float** respectively.

The standard arithmetic operators used by Python are **+**, **-**, * (multiply), **/** (divide) and ******
for exponentiation (e.g. $8 = 2^3$ or 2 ** 3). The normal rules of precedence hold, and you
can use parentheses to force the order of calculation. Two other useful operators are
% and **//**. **%** (**mod** in some programming languages) returns the remainder when one
integer is divided by another, and // (**div** in some languages) performs integer division,
discarding any remainder without rounding. So 19 % 5 = 4 and 19 // 5 = 3.

Note that the result of dividing two numbers, whether they are integer or floating point,
always results in a floating point answer.

```
>>> 3+5*2
13
>>> (3+5)*2
16
>>> 4**3
64
>>> 12/4
3.0
>>> 13/4
3.25
>>> 4.53+7.82
12.350000000000001
>>>17//6
2
>>> 17%6
5
```

Q1 Write Python statements to display the results of the following calculations:
(a) 10*6 + 5*3
(b) 10*(6 + 5)*3
(c) The remainder when 33 is divided by 7

Rounding a result

Python printed the result of `4.53 + 7.82` as `12.350000000000001`.

Because computers work in binary and not decimal, this sort of rounding error often
occurs when working with floating point numbers (i.e. numbers with a decimal point).
To print an answer to a given number of decimal places, use the `round()` function.

```
>>> result = 4.53 + 7.82
>>> roundedResult = round(result,2)
>>> roundedResult
12.35
```

Q2 Write statements to divide 6.7 by 3 and show the result to 3 decimal places.

Relational and logical operators

A **Boolean** data type can be either **True** or **False**. Operators fall into two categories: relational operators such as **>**, **==** (equal) and **!=** (not equal), and logical operators **and**, **or**, **not**.

The following table shows all the relational and logical operators.

Operation name	Operator
Less than	<
Greater than	>
Less than or equal	<=
Greater than or equal	>=
Equal	==
Not equal	!=
Logical and	and
Logical or	or
Logical not	not

Table 1.1: Relational and logical operators

```
>>> 18 == 6*3
True
>>> 18 == 6/3
False
>>> (5 > 2) and (7 > 6)
True
>>> (6 < 8) or (7 < 5)
True
```

Note that extra spaces in a statement are ignored, but are often used to aid legibility.

Naming objects

Strings, integers and floating point numbers are all **objects** in Python. Very often we need to name objects so that we can refer to them later. The names are called **identifiers** or **variable names**.

Names are assigned to objects using **assignment statements**.

A valid name, or identifier, can contain only letters, numbers and the underscore character, and cannot start with a number. An assignment statement has the variable name on the left-hand side of an = sign, and the value to be assigned on the right-hand side.

```
>>> length = 4
>>> width = 3
>>> area = length * width
>>> perimeter = 2 * (length + width)
>>> area
12
>>> perimeter
14
>>> print("Area =", area)
Area = 12
```

Guidelines for naming variables

Using meaningful variable names will help you to create programs which are easy to follow, contain fewer errors and are easier for you or someone else to amend at a later date. Here are a few tips:

- Use the standard naming conventions or traditions for Python. For example, variable names should begin with a lowercase letter. If you define a constant, such as PI or VAT, use all uppercase letters for the name. That way you will know not to change their value in a program.

- Use meaningful, descriptive names; length, width, area rather than x, y, z.

- Don't make the names too long, and use "camel caps" to separate parts of a name. For example, passMark, maxMark, averageMark.

- Note that variable names are case-sensitive, so AverageMark is a different variable name from averageMark.

> **Q3** Choose suitable variable names in the assignment statements below.
> (a) Assign the value 25 to the highest score in a game.
> (b) Assign the name Davina to a player.
> (c) Assign the values 4.5 and 6 to the height and base of a triangle. Calculate and print the area of the triangle, using the formula ½ (base x height).

Augmented assignment operators

These operators provide a quick way of writing assignment statements.

Operator	Example	Equivalent to
+=	score += 1	score = score + 1
-=	score -= losses	score = score - losses
*=	score *= 2	score = score * 2
/=	score /= total	score = score / total
%=	score %= 7	score = score % 7
//=	score //= 7	score = score // 7

Q4 Write statements using augmented assignment operators to do the following:

(a) add 1 to counter

(b) Double a variable called housePrice

(c) Subtract a variable called penalty from a variable called hits

(d) Divide totalCostOfMeal by 3.

The print statement

You have already seen the print statement, which is used to display text and data on the screen.

Using a comma as a separator

You can use a comma to separate strings or variables:

```
>>> length = 15
>>> print("The length is", length, "metres")
The length is 15 metres
```

Using a comma has the advantage that you do not have to worry about the variable type. You can mix integers, floating point numbers and strings in the print statement. However, you cannot control the spacing. One space character is automatically inserted between the output arguments of a print statement.

```
>>> cost = 15
>>> print("The cost is £", cost)
The cost is £ 15
```

Note: In some Python IDEs, the £ sign is not recognised and will cause the program to crash.

Using + as a separator

Instead of using a comma, you can use a + sign to concatenate strings in the output. However, you cannot join a string to an integer or real number, so you first have to convert any numbers to strings.

```
>>> cost = 15
>>> print("The cost is £" + cost)
Traceback (most recent call last):
    File "<pyshell#16>", line 1, in <module>
        print("The cost is £" + cost)
TypeError: must be str, not int
```

To convert a number to a string, you use the `str()` function. This is discussed in more detail in the next chapter. (See *Converting between strings and numbers*.)

You need to re-enter the statement as:

```
>>> print("The cost is £" + str(cost))
The cost is £15
```

Escape sequences

Escape sequences allow you to put special characters such as a **newline** or **tab** into your strings.

Inserting a new line

\n skips to a new line

```
>>> print("\nHello")

Hello
>>> print("\n\nGoodbye\n")


Goodbye

>>>
```

Inserting a tab character

Assume `length = 4`, `width = 3` and `area = 12`. \t inserts a tab character

```
>>> print("\t\tColumn1" + "\t\tColumn2" + "\t\tColumn3")
            Column1          Column2          Column3
>>> print("\t\t", length, "\t\t", width, "\t\t", area)
            4                3                12
```

Note: Another method of formatting output is given in Chapter 10.

Printing two outputs on the same line

To avoid printing on a new line, add `end` `=` `" "` to the end of the `print` statement, so for example:

```
print("This should all print", end = " ")
print("on the same line")  will output

This should all print on the same line
```

Note: You cannot show this in Python's Interactive mode, but you will sometimes need the end = " " parameter when you start writing programs. Whatever you put between the quote marks, in this case a space, will be printed.

(a) Write a statement to display "More pain, more gain".

(b) Write a statement to display "That's true!".

(c) Write a statement to concatenate two strings "Pelham" and "123" and display the result.

(d) What will be displayed when you enter the following on three lines?

```
print("How will this",
      "statement",
      "be printed?")
```

Try it out.

Writing a multi-line statement

The last question demonstrates that you can split a statement over several lines, so long as you don't split it inside the quote marks.

If you do need to split a line within quote marks, type a backslash (\) at the end of the first line, press `Enter` and continue writing on the next line.

```
>>> print("This is a long line of text \
split in the middle of the quote")
This is a long line of text split in the middle of the quote
```

Outside quote marks, additional spaces between variables or operators are ignored.

Triple-quoted strings

Enclosing a string in triple quotes (either single or double quotes) allows you to retain the formatting of the string, for example if it extends over several lines. Try the following example in IDLE:

```
>>> print("""
John Smith
23 Elm Street
Andover
""")

John Smith
23 Elm Street
Andover
```

The `input` statement

The input statement is used to accept input from the user, and assign the input to a variable on the left-hand side of an assignment statement. It can be used with or without a prompt to tell the user what to do. (The prompt can be provided using a print statement in the line above. Both these techniques are shown below.)

```
>>> firstName = input("Please enter your first name: ")
Please enter your first name: Martha
>>> print("Please enter your surname: ")
Please enter your surname:
>>> surname = input()
Harris
>>> print("Full name is", firstName, surname)
Full name is Martha Harris
```

Note that the `input()` statement is always followed by parentheses even if there is no prompt. In this case, you will not see any text as a prompt for input – Python will just wait until something is typed.

Mixing strings and variables in an input statement

You can use the + sign to include a variable in an input statement.

```
>>> phoneNumber = input(firstName + ", " + "please enter \
your phone number: ")
Martha, please enter your phone number:
```

You must remember to convert any numbers to strings:

```
>>> q = 3
>>> answer3 = input("Enter the answer to question " + str(q) +
": ")
Enter the answer to question 3: (Waits for user to enter data)
```

Exercises

1. (a) Write statements to prompt a user to input their favourite food and favourite colour, and display this information in the format "My favourite food is xxxx and my favourite colour is yyyy", using + symbols to concatenate the separate strings.

   (b) Display the same information using the comma separator instead of + symbols.

2. (a) Write statements to ask the user to enter their name and telephone number and then print this information on two separate lines, with a blank line in between.

   (b) Print the name and telephone number on the same line, separated by a tab character.

3. Write statements to:

   (a) perform the integer division of 40 by 11

   (b) find the remainder when 40 is divided by 11

   (c) calculate 2^{10}

   (d) test whether "three" is greater than "two"

   (e) test whether "abc" is less than than "ABC"

   (f) test whether (1<=4 and 7<=7) is True

   (g) find the result of the Boolean condition equivalent to: "Fred" not equal to "fred"

Chapter 2
Strings and numbers

Objectives

- write and execute programs in script mode
- learn some useful string methods and functions
- convert string input to numerical values and vice versa
- identify and correct syntax errors

Script mode

In the last chapter we used **interactive mode**, which allows you to test out different Python statements and gives instant feedback. However, if you want to save a program so that you can load and run it later, you need to use **script mode**. Alternatively, you can use one of the many interactive development environments (IDEs) that are available to create, edit, save and run Python programs. In this book the screenshots show programs entered and executed in Python IDLE.

2

You can open an **Editor window** in Python's IDLE (integrated development environment) from the interactive Shell window. Select *File, New File* from the menu bar, and a new window will open. In this window, type a one-line program:

```
print("Hello World")
```

- Before you can run the program, you must save it, so select *File, Save* from the menu bar and save it with the name **hello world.py** in a suitable folder
- Then select *Run, Run Module* from the menu or use the shortcut key F5
- The interactive window will appear with the result:

```
Hello World
```

You can leave the interactive window open while you are writing programs in script mode. That way, if you are not sure about a statement, you can try it before writing it in your program.

Adding comments

It's a good idea to include comments at the top of every program (beyond the very trivial) that you write, giving the name and purpose of the program, your name and the date you wrote the program. You may also want to document in which folder you have saved it so you can quickly find it again after a few weeks or months.

Within the program, add comments to explain the purpose of any tricky bit of code and how it works.

To write a comment, type the # symbol. Anything to the right of # will be ignored.

Keeping the console window open

If you run the Python program by double-clicking its name in your folder, rather than launching it from IDLE, the program will run and then the console window will immediately close so that you can't see what happened. To keep it open, add a line to the end of your program:

```
input ("\nPress Enter to exit: ")
```

The window will remain open until the user presses the **Enter** key.

String methods

Every data type in Python is an **object**. Strings, integers and floating point numbers are all objects, and they have built-in **methods** which perform useful tasks. Some useful string methods are shown in Table 2.1.

Method	Example	Description
upper	astring.upper()	returns astring all in uppercase
lower	astring.lower()	returns astring all in lowercase
index	astring.index(item)	returns the index of the first occurrence of item in astring, or an error if not found
find	astring.find(item)	returns the index of the first occurrence of item in astring, or -1 if not found
replace	astring.replace(old,new)	replaces all occurrences of old substring with new in astring

Table 2.1: String methods

Every character in a string may be referred to using its **index** or position in the string. The first character in a string `myString` is referred to as `myString[0]`.

Below is a program which uses some of the string methods. It must be saved before you can run it. All the programs given in the text as examples and exercises may be downloaded from **www.pgonline.co.uk**.

Example 1

```
#Program name: Ch 2 Example 1 string methods.py
#Tests string methods

astring = "You've done a good job"
print("Original string:",astring)
print("Uppercase string:",astring.upper())
print("New String:",astring.replace("good","brilliant"))
print("Original string:",astring)
print("The word 'done' starts at index",astring.index("done"))
```

When you run the program, the output appears in the Python Shell window:

```
Original string: You've done a good job
Uppercase string: YOU'VE DONE A GOOD JOB
New String: You've done a brilliant job
Original string: You've done a good job
The word 'done' starts at index 7
```

Notice that the original string is left unchanged. If you want to save the changed string, you could write, for example:

```
bstring = astring.upper()
```

or:

```
astring = astring.upper()
```

Syntax errors

If you make any mistakes when entering Python statements, the computer will report a syntax error.

Example 2

Some errors have been inserted into the program in Example 1.

The Python interpreter looks at the lines one by one and as soon as it encounters a syntax error, it will stop and give you a message "Invalid syntax".

```
File  Edit  Format  Run  Options  Window  Help
#Program name: Ch 2 Example 2 string methods.py
#Tests string methods

astring = "You've done a good job"
print("\nOriginal string:" astring)
print("\nUppercase string:", astring.upper)
print("\nNew String:",astring.replace("good","excellent")
print("\nOriginal string:",astring)
```

SyntaxError   ✕

    ✕   invalid syntax

                                    OK

There is a missing comma before the variable name `astring`. You can click OK, correct the error, resave and try again.

Q1 There are two more errors in the program. Can you spot them?

Inputting numbers

A simple program to find the cost of lunch is shown below.

Example 3

```
#Program name: Ch 2 Example 3 Cost of lunch.py
main = 3.00
juice = 0.75
banana = 1.00
total = main + juice + banana
print("Total for lunch: ",total)
```

This prints out

```
Total for lunch: 4.75
```

Example 4

To make the program more useful, we could ask the user to enter the cost of the main course, juice and banana. Here is a first attempt:

```
#Program name: Ch 2 Example 4 Cost of lunch v2.py
main = input("Enter cost of main course: ")
juice = input("Enter cost of juice: ")
banana = input("Enter cost of banana: ")
total = main + juice + banana
print("Total for lunch: ",total)
```

When you run this program, the output could be (depending on what the user inputs):

```
Enter cost of main course: 4.00
Enter cost of juice: .50
Enter cost of banana: 1
Total for lunch: 4.00.501
```

What has happened is that Python has treated each of the inputs as strings, not numbers, and concatenated the strings instead of adding the numbers.

Converting between strings and numbers

Whenever you input numerical values, you have to convert from `string` to `integer` or `float`. Here are some useful conversion functions:

Function	Description	Example	Returns
float(x)	converts a string to a floating point value	float("4.65")	4.65
int(x)	converts a string to an integer	int("3")	3
str(x)	Converts a number x to a string value	str(5.0)	'5.0'

Table 2.2: Type conversion functions

Example 5

You can do the conversion in the same line as the input statement:

```
#Program name: Ch 2 Example 5 Cost of lunch v3.py
main = float(input("Enter cost of main course: "))
juice = float(input("Enter cost of juice: "))
banana = float(input("Enter cost of banana: "))
total = main + juice + banana
print("Total for lunch: ",total)
```

This produces the following output:

```
Enter cost of main course: 4.00
Enter cost of juice: .50
Enter cost of banana: 1
Total for lunch: 5.5
```

Formatting output is covered in Chapter 9, pages 68-69. An explanation is left until then; however, if you change the last line of the program to

```
print("%-16s%5.2f" %("Total for lunch:",total))
```

the 16-character text is left-justified, five characters with 2 characters after the decimal point are allowed for the variable total and the output will appear as

```
Total for lunch: 5.50
```

Functions and methods

Note the different ways in which functions and methods are written. A **method** is written using the dot notation, with the name of the object followed by a full-stop and then the method name:

```
posa = astring.find("a")
```

Finding the length of a string

A **function** is written with the function name followed by the name of the object in parentheses. The example below shows a useful function to find the number of characters in a string:

```
numchars = len(astring)
```

In Chapter 8 you will learn how to write your own functions. Built-in methods are used in this book, but you will not need to create your own methods until you start object-oriented programming, which is not covered in this textbook.

Exercises

1. Write a program to do the following:

    -   assign the string "A picture's worth a thousand words" to `proverb`
    -   replace "A picture's" with "An image is" and assign the new string to `proverbImage`
    -   find the first occurrence of the letter "o" in the original string and assign the value of the index to `firstO`
    -   convert the original string to uppercase and assign it to `proverbUpper`
    -   find the number of characters in the string.
    -   display the results of all these operations, as well as the original string.

2. Write a program to ask the user to enter the radius of a circle and print out the area, πr^2 and the circumference, $2\pi r$. ($\pi = 3.14159$)

3. Write a program which asks the user to type in two floating point numbers `num1` and `num2`, then rounds and prints their sum and product to the specified number of decimal places:

    ```
    The sum of num1 and num2 is nnnn.nn
    The product of num1 and num2 is nnnn.nnn
    ```

    For example:

    ```
    The sum of 3.453 and 2.1 is 5.55
    The product of 3.453 and 2.1 is 7.251
    ```

Chapter 3
Selection

Objectives

- Learn to write conditional statements using Boolean expressions
- Write selection statements using `if`, `else`, `elif`
- Use nested if statements
- Use complex Boolean expressions involving `and`, `or` and `not`
- Import a Python library module and use the `randint()` function to generate random numbers

Programming constructs

3

There are three basic ways of controlling the order in which program statements are carried out:

- Sequence
- Selection
- Iteration

In the previous two chapters we wrote program statements one after the other in the order in which they were to be executed. This is the **sequence** programming construct.

In this chapter we will use **selection** statements to control program flow. These statements all start with the keyword `if`, followed by a condition to be tested. For example:

```
if shape == "circle":
    area = PI * r**2
else:
    area = length * breadth
```

Note the semi-colons at the end of the `if` and `else` conditions, and the indentation of statements following each of these lines, all of which are mandatory.

Boolean conditions

The following **Boolean conditions** may be used in `if` statements:

==	equal to
!=	not equal to
>	greater than
>=	greater than or equal
<	less than
<=	less than or equal

Q1 Write Python statements to input two numbers and assign the smaller of the two to a variable called `minimum`.

Using a Boolean variable in a condition statement

A **Boolean variable** can only take the value **True** or **False**. So for example we could write a conditional statement such as:

```
IF amount < 10 THEN
    validAmount = True
```

and later in the program the Boolean variable `validAmount` could be tested:

```
if validAmount == True:
    print("This is a valid amount")
```

However, the statement can also be written more simply as:

```
if validAmount:
    print("This is a valid amount")
```

The `elif` clause

This is useful if there are several possible routes through the program depending on the value of a variable.

Example 1

Students are assigned a grade of A, B, C or F depending on the average mark they have achieved over a number of assignments.

Mark of 75 or more: A

Mark of 60 – 74:   B

Mark of 50 – 59:   C

Mark less than 50:   F

Write a statement to assign the grade to a variable `grade` depending on the value of `mark`.

```
if mark >= 75:
    grade = "A"
elif mark >= 60:
    grade = "B"
elif mark >= 50:
    grade = "C"
else:
    grade = "F"
```

A particular `elif` is tested only when all previous `if` and `elif` statements are False. When one `if` or `elif` is True, all subsequent tests are skipped.

Nested selection statements

If there is more than one condition to be tested, you can use a nested selection statement.

Example 2

A firm hiring new employees requires all applicants to take an aptitude test. If they pass the test, they are interviewed and if they pass the interview, they are offered employment. If they fail the interview, they are rejected. If they fail the aptitude test, they are given the opportunity to resit the test at a future date.

```
if testResult == "Pass":
    if interviewOK:
        print("Hired")
    else:
        print("Rejected")
else THEN
    print("Resit test")
```

Complex Boolean expressions

Boolean expressions may include `and`, `or` or `not`.

Operator	Description
and	Returns True if both conditions are true
or	Returns True if either or both conditions are true
not	A true expression becomes False and vice versa

Example 3

Here are some complex Boolean expressions used in `if` statements:

(a) `if day == "Saturday" or day == "Sunday":`
    `weekendRate = True`

(b) `if (not day == "Saturday") and (not day == "Sunday"):`
    `weekendRate = False`

(c) `if (testResult == "Pass") and (interviewOK):`
    `print("Hired")`
  `else:`
    `print("Rejected")`

Q2 In (b) above, assume `weekendRate` is initially set to `False` and `day = Sunday`. What will `weekendRate` be set to?

Importing library modules

In Chapter 2 we used some built-in functions such as `int`, `str` and `float`. In addition to these built-in functions, Python has a library of useful modules such as `datetime`, `time`, `random`, `sqlite3`, `tkinter`, `pdb` (a debugging module) which can be imported into a program.

Generating a random number

The `randint()` function generates a random number. It is a function included in the `random` module and to use it, you must first import the module by including the statement

```
import random
```

at the start of the program. This imports the module called `random`. Then in your program, to generate a random integer between a range of integers a and b you write

```
num = random.randint(a,b)
```

Example 4

Generate two random numbers between 1 and 6 to represent the throw of two dice. If the numbers are equal, print, for example, "You threw a double 5"

```
die1 = random.randint(1,6)
die2 = random.randint(1,6)
if die1 == die2:
    print("You threw a double", die1)
else:
    print("Not a double:", die1, die2)
```

Exercises

1. Write a program to allow the user to enter the length and width of a rectangle and calculate the area. If the length and width are equal, print "`This is a square of area nn.nn`". Otherwise, print "`This is a rectangle of area nn.nn`".

2. Write a program to display a menu of options:

    ```
    Menu
    1.  Music
    2.  History
    3.  Design and Technology
    4.  Exit
    Please enter your choice:
    ```

    The user then enters a choice and the program prints a message such as "`You chose History`". If they choose option 4, the program prints "`Goodbye`".

3. Write a program to simulate the throw of two dice (each between 1 and 6). Print the numbers representing the two throws.

    If the numbers on the two dice are not equal, the player's score is the sum of the numbers thrown. Print the score.

    If the numbers on the two dice are equal, the player scores twice the sum of the number thrown. Print "You threw a double", and the score.

4. Write a program to input the value of goods purchased in a shop. A discount is subtracted from the value to find the amount owed.

    If the value is £200 or more, 10% discount is given.

    If the value is between £100 and £199.99, 5% discount is given.

    Print the value of goods, discount given and amount owed.

5. Write a program to calculate car park charges. Up to 2 hours costs £3.50, up to 4 hours £5.00, up to 12 hours £10.00. The driver enters the number of hours they require and the machine prints the current time, expiry time and charge. For example:

    ```
    Time now:   Wed Mar 8 15:47:46 2017
    Expires:    Thu Mar 9 03:47:46 2017
    Charge = 10.00
    ```

    Tip: Use the Python library function `time` by writing `import time` at the top of the program. The time in seconds since January 1st 1970 is given by

    ```
    currentTime = time.time()
    ```

    This can be formatted as shown in the sample output above with the statement:

    ```
    currentTimeFormatted = time.ctime(currentTime)
    ```

3

Chapter 4

Iteration

Objectives

- Use `for` loops (definite iteration)
- Use `while` loops (indefinite iteration)
- use string functions and operators

The `for` loop

Sometimes in a program, you want to repeat a sequence of steps a certain number of times. A `for` loop can iterate over a sequence of numbers in a range in different ways. For example, the programmer can specify that a number used as a counter has a range `a..b`, meaning from `a` up to but not including `b`.

Example 1

```
#Program name: Ch 4 Example 1 For loop examples.py
# Sample range 1: print the numbers 1 to 5
print("Numbers from 1-5:")
for number in range (1,6):
    print(number, end = " ")


#Sample range 2: print numbers 0 to 4
print("\nNumbers from 0-4:" )
for number in range (5):
    print(number, end = " ")


#Sample range 3: print every third number from 1 to 16
print("\nEvery third number in range 1-16:" )
for number in range (1,17,3):
    print(number, end = " ")
```

```
#Sample range 4: print every number from 5 down to to 1
print ("\nEvery number from 5 down to 1:" )
for number in range (5,0,-1):
    print (number, end = " ")
```

The output is:

```
Numbers from 1-5:
1 2 3 4 5
Numbers from 0-4:
0 1 2 3 4
Every third number from 1-16:
1 4 7 10 13 16
Every number from 5 down to 1:
5 4 3 2 1
```

Note the following points in the sample ranges:

- **Sample range 1** shows that if you want the range to go from 1 to 5, you must specify the range as `range (1, 6)`. The range will start with the first number specified, and go **up to but not including** the second number specified.

- **Sample range 2** shows that if you specify only one value in the range, this is taken as the end of the range. The first value in the range defaults to 0. Thus `range (5)` includes the five values 0, 1, 2, 3, 4.

- **Sample range 3** shows that you can count in threes. You can increment the counter by any integer value.

- **Sample range 4** shows that you can increment the counter by a negative value. The counter will then count down from the first value specified. It will not include the last number in the specified range.

(See Chapter 5 for an alternative and powerful way of specifying the range at the start of a `for` loop.)

Nested loops

You can have one loop "nested" inside another. The next example shows how you could print all the multiplication tables from 2 to 10.

Example 2

```
#Program name: Ch 4 Example 2 Multiplication tables.py

for table in range (2,11):
    print ("\n" + str (table) + " Times Table ")
    for n in range (2,13):
        print (str (table) + " x " + str (n)+ " = " + str (table * n))
```

23

> **Q1** Write Python code to do the following:
>
> (a) Print the numbers 10 - 0 starting at 10. Then print "Lift-off!" Import the `time` module at the start of the program with the statement `import time`. Include a time delay of 1 second before printing each number, using the statement `time.sleep(1)`.
>
> (b) Ask the user to enter 5 numbers. Keep a running total and print the total and average of the numbers.

The `while` loop

The `while` loop is used when the number of times the loop will be performed is initially unknown. The loop is performed as long as a specified Boolean condition is **True**. If the condition is **False** before the `while` statement is encountered, the loop will be skipped.

The Boolean condition is tested in the `while` statement at the start of the loop, and again each time the loop is completed. If it becomes **True** halfway through the loop, the remaining statements in the loop will be executed before the condition is re-tested.

Example 3

Write code to accept a series of integer test results from a user, find and print the maximum and minimum results. Assume all the results are between 0 and 100. The end of the input is signalled by an input of -1.

```
#Program name: Ch 4 Example 3 max and min.py
testResult = int(input("Please enter test result: "))
# Set maximum and minimum to first test result
maxResult = testResult
minResult = testResult

while testResult != -1:
   if testResult > maxResult:
      maxResult = testResult
   if testResult < minResult:
      minResult = testResult
   testResult = int(input("Please enter test result (-1 to
   finish): "))

print("\nMaximum test result =", maxResult)
print("Minimum test result =", minResult)
```

The output will be similar to this:

```
Please enter test result: 45
Please enter test result (-1 to finish): 63
Please enter test result (-1 to finish): 24
Please enter test result (-1 to finish): 33
Please enter test result (-1 to finish): 45
Please enter test result (-1 to finish): -1

Maximum test result = 63
Minimum test result = 24
```

Note carefully the technique of writing the first input statement **before** entering the `while` loop. This value is then processed and subsequent input statements are executed at the end of the loop, so that as soon as -1 is input, the next thing that happens is that the condition is tested and the loop is exited.

Q2 What would be the result of setting `maxResult = 0, minResult = 100, testResult = 0` at the start of the program, and having just one `input` statement as the first statement in the loop?

Q3 The original program is altered so that the input is not converted from string to integer, and the condition to be tested is `testResult! = "-1"`. What will be output if the values 34, 19, 100, 56, -1 are input? Explain your answer.

Q4 Amend the program so that if the user enters -1 as the first input, the output will be "No results input".

String processing

Loops are often used when processing strings. In the example below, the `for` loop condition is written in an alternative way so that each character in the string is processed.

Recall from Chapter 2, page 16, that the function `len(string)` returns the number of characters in a string.

Example 4

Count and print the number of words and the number of characters in a piece of text. You can count words by counting the number of spaces in the text, and adding 1 to the total. (This assumes there is exactly one space between each word.)

```
#Program name: Ch 4 Example 4 words in sentence
sentence = input("Enter a sentence: ")
numWords = 1
for letter in sentence:
    if letter == " ":
        numWords += 1
print("Number of words =", numWords)
print("Number of characters =", len(sentence))
```

Indexing strings

Each character in a string can be referenced by its **index**, starting at 0. Thus, if a variable called word contains the characters "python", word[0] = "p", word[1] = y", word[2] = "t" and so on.

Example 5

Find the index of the first occurrence of the letter "e" in a sentence input by the user.

In this example, we will make use of the "break" statement. This breaks out of the loop, transferring control to the first statement after the loop. Although this is sometimes considered by some to be bad practice in structured programming, others disagree and it often simplifies the code.

```
#Program name: Ch 4 Example 5 first e.py
eIndex = -1
sentence = input("Please enter a sentence: ")
for ePosition in range(len(sentence)):
    if sentence[ePosition] == "e":
        eIndex = ePosition
        print("Index of first 'e' is ", eIndex)
        break

if eIndex == -1:
    print("There is no 'e' in the sentence.")
```

Q5 Recall from Chapter 2 that the string method astring.find(item) returns the index of the first occurrence of item in astring, or −1 if not found. Use this to code an alternative program which has the same input and output as the program above.

Slicing strings

Using indexing, you can isolate a single character in a string. Using slicing, you can isolate anything from a single character to the whole string, so for example you could look at the first three characters of a car registration number, or the middle five characters of a nine character string.

Example 6

You can try out various slices using an interactive session.

```
>>> name = "Phillip"
>>> nickname = name[0:5]
>>> print(nickname)
>>> Phill
>>> print(name[1:5])
>>> hill
```

With both indexing and slicing, you can use negative numbers. Sometimes it makes more sense to start counting position numbers from the end of a string. You can visualise the end points with alternative numberings as shown in the figure below:

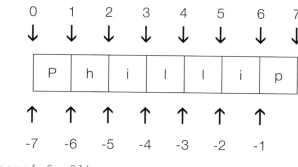

```
>>> print(name[-6:-3])
hil
```

If you specify an impossible slice, where the starting point is bigger than the end point, like name[3:1] or name[4:-5], Python will return an empty string.

```
>>> impossible = name[5:1]
>>> impossible
''
```

However, you can mix positive and negative end points:

```
>>> print(name[-6:4])
hil
```

Interrupting execution

Sometimes a logic error may result in a program looping endlessly. You can terminate (kill) a running program by selecting *Shell*, *Interrupt execution* from the menu bar in the Python Shell menu, or by pressing the shortcut key combination **Ctrl-C**.

Example 7

In the following example, the programmer has forgotten to write an `input` statement at the end of the `while` loop.

```
#Program name: Ch 4 Example 7 endless loop.py
print("\nThis program demonstrates how you can get into an
endless loop")
print("\nYou can stop it by selecting Shell, Interrupt
Execution")
print("from the menu in the Python Shell window.\n")

name = input("Enter a name, xxx to end: ")
while name != "xxx":
    print("Number of letters in name:",len(name))
```

The output will be something like:

```
Number of letters in name:  9
Number of letters in name:  9
Number of letters in name:  9
```

... (endlessly repeated)

Exercises

1. Write a program to generate 10 random numbers between 1 and 10, and print out the 10 numbers and the total of the numbers.

2. Extend the program in Exercise 1 to repeat the generation of 10 random numbers 1000 times. Do not print out the random numbers or the total of each set of 10 numbers – just print the average of the totals at the end of the program. Is the answer what you would expect?

3. Write a program to allow the user to enter a number of 5-character product codes, beginning with the letters "AB" or "AS" followed by 3 numeric characters.

    Count and print the total number of product codes starting with "AB" and the total number of product codes ending in "00".

    Test your program by entering product codes AS123, AS101, AB111, AB345, CD222, AB200.

Chapter 5
Lists and tuples

Objectives

- Understand why lists are useful
- declare a list and use list functions and methods
- use one- and two-dimensional lists to solve problems
- distinguish between lists and tuples

Python lists

A **list** in Python is a type of sequence, like a string. However, unlike a string, which can contain only characters, a list can contain elements of any type. A list could contain, for example, several names:

```
name = ["Mark", "Juan", "Ali", "Cathy", "Sylvia", "Noah"]
```

These names can be indexed, just like the elements of a string, so
`name[0] = "Mark"`, `name[5] = "Noah"`.

A list can hold elements of different types, so for example you could define a list like this:

```
score = ["Ben Charlton",14,17,16,15,17]
```

Defining a list

A list may be defined in a Python program as in the examples above. You can also define an empty list, or a list with many elements of the same value, as shown in the interactive session below:

```
>>> aList = []
>>> aList
[]
>>> bList = [None] * 10
>>> bList
```

```
[None, None, None, None, None, None, None, None, None, None]
>>> cList = [0]*5
>>> cList
[0, 0, 0, 0, 0]
```

`None` is a special value in Python which acts as a useful placeholder for a value. It evaluates to `False` when tested in a conditional statement.

Operations on lists

Some list methods are shown in the table below. Assume `a = [45,13,19,13,8]`

List operation	Description	Example	List contents following execution	Return value
isEmpty()	Test for empty list	a.isEmpty()	[45, 13, 19, 13, 8]	False
append(item)	Add a new item to list to the end of the list	a.append(33)	[45, 13, 19, 13, 8, 33]	
remove(item)	Remove the first occurrence of an item from list	a.remove(13)	[45, 19, 13, 8, 33]	
len()	Return the number of items	len(a)	[45, 19, 13, 8, 33]	5
index(item)	Return the position of item	a.index(8)	[45, 19, 13, 8, 33]	3
insert(pos,item)	Insert a new item at position pos	a.insert(2,7)	[45, 19, 7, 13, 8, 33]	
pop()	Remove and return the last item in the list	a.pop()	[45, 19, 7, 13, 8]	33
pop(pos)	Remove and return the item at position pos	a.pop(1)	[45, 7, 13, 8]	19

Note that `len ()` is a **function**, not a **method**, and is written in a different way.

Example 1

Determine whether the number `100` is in the list `listB = [56,78,100,45,88,71]`, and if so, print its index.

```
#Program name: Ch 5 Example 1 list of numbers.py
listB = [56,78,100,45,88,71]
if 100 in listB:
    print("100 is at position ", listB.index(100))
else:
    print("100 is not in the list")
```

Example 2

Write code to print the numbers in `listB` on separate lines

```
for num in listB:
    print(num)
```

Alternatively, you could write

```
for index in range(len(listB)):
    print(listB[index])
```

> **Q1** What will happen if you write
> ```
> for index in range(7):
>     print(listB[index])
> ```

Appending to a list

A list is a fixed size; you cannot, for example, add a new item to `listB` by writing

```
listB[6] = 81
```

You will get an "index out of range" error.

Instead, you must use the `append` method, defined in the table on the previous page.

```
listB.append(81)
```

This will result in `listB` being set equal to `[56,78,100,45,88,71,81]`

You can append one list to another. If you want to concatenate (join together) two lists `numList1` and `numList2`, you can use the augmented operator `+=` . The following interactive session shows this:

```
>>> numList1 = [1,2,3,4]
>>> numList2 = [5,6,7,8]
>>> numList1 += numList2
>>> numList1
>>> [1,2,3,4,5,6,7,8]
```

Alternatively, write

```
numList1 = numList1 + numList2
```

> **Q2** Concatenate the two lists `list1`, equal to `[2,4,6,8,10]` and `list2`, equal to `[1,3,5,7,9,11,13]` to create a new list `list3`.

> **Q3** Remove the last element from `list1` and assign it to a variable `last`.

5

Q4 Create a new list called `list4` by slicing `list3`, so that `list4` contains the four elements indexed 3 to 6 of `list3`.

List processing

Items are often held in lists for further processing. The items may be input by the user or read from a file on disk, for example. Sometimes the list of values may be defined in the program.

Example 3

Define a list containing the names of students in a class. Ask the user to input the exam results for each student. Print a report showing the data with column headings

```
Student       Exam mark
```

At the end of the report, print the name of the student with the highest mark, and the mark obtained.

In the following program, names have been padded with spaces to enable printing in neat columns using the **tab** escape sequence \t.

```
#Program name: Ch 5 Example 3 exam results.py
#program prints list of exam results and highest result.

studentNames = ["Khan, Afridi     ", "Milner, Angela    ",
"Philips, Justine", "Osmani, Pias     "]
results = []
topMark = 0
numberOfStudents = len(studentNames)

for student in range(numberOfStudents):
    print("Enter mark for",studentNames[student],": ",end = " ")
    mark = int(input())
    results.append(mark)
    if mark > topMark:
        topMark = mark
        topStudent = studentNames[student]

print("\nStudent\t\t\tExam mark")
for student in range(numberOfStudents):
    print(studentNames[student],"\t",results[student])

print("\nTop result: ",topStudent,topMark)
```

This produces output in the format:

```
Enter mark for Khan, Afridi      :   56
Enter mark for Milner, Angela    :   67
Enter mark for Philips, Justine  :   71
Enter mark for Osmani, Pias      :   52

Student                 Exam mark
Khan, Afridi               56
Milner, Angela             67
Philips, Justine           71
Osmani, Pias               52

Top result:   Philips, Justine  71
```

Two-dimensional lists

In some applications you may need a table of values rather than a one-dimensional list. Suppose you wanted to hold the data in the following table, which shows the average maximum and minimum temperatures (°C) in London for each month of the year.

Month	Max temp (°C)	Min temp (°C)
January	6	3
February	7	3
March	10	4
April	13	6
May	17	9
June	20	12
July	22	14
August	21	14
September	19	12
October	14	9
November	10	6
December	7	3

These values could be stored in a two-dimensional list named `monthlyAvg`:

```
monthlyAvg = [   ["January",6,3],
                 ["February",7,3],
                 ["March",10,4],
and so on down to
                 ["December",7,3]   ]
```

Each element of the two-dimensional list is referred to by two indices giving the row index (between 0 and 11) and column index (between 0 and 2).

The average maximum temperature in March would be referred to as `monthlyAvg[2][1]`.

The data for March is `["March",10,4]` and is held in `monthlyAvg[2]`.

Q5 How would you refer to the average minimum temperature for November?

Q6 Write a statement to print the data for December, giving the month and the two temperatures as a list in the format `[monthname, maxtemp, mintemp]`.

Q7 What will be printed by the following statements?
(a) `print(len(monthlyAvg))`
(b) `print(len(monthlyAvg[4])`

Example 4

Write a program to enable a user to enter the average maximum and minimum temperatures for each month and store them in a two-dimensional list named `monthlyAvg`. Print the monthly data when it has all been entered.

Some things to note about this program:

- The month names are supplied in a list so that the user does not have to enter them.
- The table `monthlyAvg` which will hold the monthly averages is initialised to an empty list. It will eventually contain 12 elements, each element being a list of 3 elements.
- The three values in each row (`monthName[m]`, maximum and minimum) have been assigned to a list variable called `row`, which is then appended to the table `monthlyAvg`.
- Recall that adding `end = " "` to the end of a `print` statement means that one space will be printed at the end of the line, and the next `print` statement will print the data on the same line.

```
"""
Program name:Ch 5 Example 4 2-D list of temperatures.py
#program to allow the user to enter monthly average maximum
and minimum temperatures
"""

monthName = ["January","February","March","April","May","June",
    "July","August","September","October","November","December"]
monthlyAvg = []

for m in range(12):
    print("Enter average maximum and minimum for " + monthName[m])
    maximum = int(input("Maximum: "))
    minimum = int(input("Minimum: "))
    row = [monthName[m], maximum, minimum]
    monthlyAvg.append(row)
#now print the list
print("\n")
for m in range(12):
    for index in range(3):
        print(monthlyAvg[m][index],end = " ")
    print("\n")
```

Tuples

Tuples are very similar to lists, with one major difference: they are **immutable**, which means that once defined, they cannot be changed. Like a list, a tuple can hold a number or items of the same or different types, can be indexed, sliced and sorted.

A tuple is written in parentheses (round brackets) rather than square brackets. The following interactive session demonstrates the immutability of a tuple.

```
>>> name = ("Hilary", "Jenny", "George", "Ben")
>>> print(name[2])
George
>>> name[2] = "Jorge"
Traceback (most recent call last):
   File "<pyshell#44>", line 1, in <module>
      name[2] = "Jorge"
TypeError: 'tuple' object does not support item assignment
```

Exercises

1. Write Python statements to:

   (a) define an empty list called `alist`

   (b) append a string element `"apple"` to `alist`

   (c) define a list named `blist` containing 20 integer elements, all zero

   (d) concatenate `alist` and `blist` and assign the result to `clist`

   (e) remove the last element of `clist` and assign it to `lastC`

2. Write a program to do the following:

   Initialise an empty list. Ask the user to input as many names as they like, until they enter "End" instead of a name. Slice the list in half and print the first half of the list. If the list contains an odd number of values, e.g. nine values, print only the first four values.

3. Write a program to accept a student name, and the marks obtained on 10 weekly tests. Print the name, average mark, top three marks and bottom three marks. (Use `sortedMarks = sorted(markList, reverse = True)` to sort the list.)

4. Extend the program shown in Example 3 to find the months with the hottest average temperature and the coldest average temperature. Print the month names and relevant temperatures of these months.

5. Write a program to simulate how the top scores of several players playing an online game many times could be held in a list.

   (a) Define a two-dimensional list which will hold in each row, a user ID and their top score for an online game. The two-dimensional list is to be initialised with the following values:

userID	topScore
AAA01	135
BBB01	87
CCC01	188
DDD01	109

   (b) Ask a user to enter their ID. Check if the user ID is in the list. If it is not found, append a new row containing the user ID and a score of zero.

   (c) Generate a random number between 50 and 200 to represent the score for this game. Locate the user. Check whether the new score is greater than the score in the list, and if so, replace it.

   (d) Print the whole list of players and scores.

   Repeat steps **b** to **d** until a user ID of xxx is entered.

Chapter 6

Validating user input

Objectives

- Understand the importance of validating user input
- Use exception handling routines in Python
- Use regular expressions to validate input data

Validating user input

Whatever a user is asked to enter, if there is any possibility that the input could cause the program to crash or give a wrong result, it should be validated.

There are different types of validation check that can be carried out, for example:

- length check
- type check
- format check

Length check

If data such as a product code input by the user should be a certain length, for example 6 characters, you can check this using the `len()` function and ask the user to re-input the data if it is invalid, until they get it right.

```python
prodCode = ""
while len(prodCode) != 6:
    prodCode = input("Please enter 6-character product code: ")
    if len(prodCode) != 6:
        print("Invalid code")
```

> **Q1** Rewrite this validation routine with the first input statement outside the `while...` loop.

Type check

Any user input is treated by default as a string, and has to be converted to an integer or floating point number by a string conversion function `int` or `float` if it is to be used in a calculation. However, if the user has entered an invalid character, the program will crash unless steps are taken to prevent this.

One method of checking that a valid number has been entered is to use the `try ... except ... else` clause. This will catch an error and prevent the program from crashing. If no error is detected, the `else` clause will be executed.

Example 1

Write a program to calculate the total and average of several numbers entered by the user. The end of the input is to be signalled by an input of end.

```
#Program name: Ch 6 Example 1 try except.py
print("This program accepts integers or real numbers\n",
      "and finds the total and average of the numbers.")
print("Enter 'end' to signal end of data entry.")
total = 0
count = 0
number = input("Please enter a number: ")
while number.lower() != "end":
    try:
        float(number)
    except ValueError:
        print("This is not a number")
    else:
        number = float(number)
        total += number
        count += 1
    number = input("Enter next number, 'end' to finish : ")
average = total/count
print("\nTotal =", total, " Average = ", round(average,2))
```

The ASCII code

The standard ASCII code uses seven bits to represent 128 different combinations of binary digits, more than enough to represent all the characters on a standard English language keyboard. The table of ASCII characters and the equivalent decimal and binary characters is shown on the next page. The first 32 characters represent non-printing characters such as *Backspace*, *Enter* and *Escape* and are not shown in the table.

ASCII	Dec	Binary	ASCII	Dec	Binary	ASCII	Dec	Binary
space	032	010 0000	@	064	100 0000	`	096	110 0000
!	033	010 0001	A	065	100 0001	a	097	110 0001
"	034	010 0010	B	066	100 0010	b	098	110 0010
#	035	010 0011	C	067	100 0011	c	099	110 0011
$	036	010 0100	D	068	100 0100	d	100	110 0100
%	037	010 0101	E	069	100 0101	e	101	110 0101
&	038	010 0110	F	070	100 0110	f	102	110 0110
'	039	010 0111	G	071	100 0111	g	103	110 0111
(	040	010 1000	H	072	100 1000	h	104	110 1000
)	041	010 1001	I	073	100 1001	i	105	110 1001
*	042	010 1010	J	074	100 1010	j	106	110 1010
+	043	010 1011	K	075	100 1011	k	107	110 1011
,	044	010 1100	L	076	100 1100	l	108	110 1100
-	045	010 1101	M	077	100 1101	m	109	110 1101
.	046	010 1110	N	078	100 1110	n	110	110 1110
/	047	010 1111	O	079	100 1111	o	111	110 1111
0	048	011 0000	P	080	101 0000	p	112	111 0000
1	049	011 0001	Q	081	101 0001	q	113	111 0001
2	050	011 0010	R	082	101 0010	r	114	111 0010
3	051	011 0011	S	083	101 0011	s	115	111 0011
4	052	011 0100	T	084	101 0100	t	116	111 0100
5	053	011 0101	U	085	101 0101	u	117	111 0101
6	054	011 0110	V	086	101 0110	v	118	111 0110
7	055	011 0111	W	087	101 0111	w	119	111 0111
8	056	011 1000	X	088	101 1000	x	120	111 1000
9	057	011 1001	Y	089	101 1001	y	121	111 1001
:	058	011 1010	Z	090	101 1010	z	122	111 1010
;	059	011 1011	[	091	101 1011	{	123	111 1011
<	060	011 1100	\	092	101 1100			124	111 1100
=	061	011 1101	]	093	101 1101	}	125	111 1101
>	062	011 1110	^	094	101 1110	~	126	111 1110
?	063	011 1111	_	095	101 1111	DEL	127	111 1111

The ASCII code

6

The functions `ord()` and `chr()`

These two functions convert between a character and the decimal representation of its ASCII value. If you try this out in the interactive window, you will see, for example:

```
>>> ord("s")
115
>>> chr(106)
'j'
>>>
```

Example 2

Ask the user to enter a new password. The password must contain at least one uppercase letter. If it does not, the user is asked to input another password.

One way of checking that a character is an uppercase letter is to convert it to ASCII and check that its decimal equivalent is between 65 and 90.

```
#Program name: Ch 6 Example 2 validate password.py
print("Password must contain at least one uppercase letter")
password = input("Please enter new password: ")
passwordValid = False
while not passwordValid:
    for index in range(len(password)):
        if ord(password[index]) in range(65,91):
            passwordValid = True
    if not passwordValid:
        password = input("Invalid - please enter new password: ")
print("Password accepted")
```

Example 3

Once the user has set a password for a particular application, they will be asked to enter it when they log on, and it will be compared with a stored password. They are typically given three attempts to get it right.

The following program shows one method of doing this. Notice the statement `break` which will cause the program to exit the `while` loop. The Boolean variable `passwordValid` acts as a **flag**, which if `False` indicates an invalid password.

```
#Program name: Ch6 Example 3 compare password.py
#Program to check a user's password
storedPassword = "Secret246"
passwordValid = False
attempt = 1
```

```
while attempt <= 3:
    password = input("Input password: ")
    if password == storedPassword:
        passwordValid = True
        break
    else:
        print("This password is not correct...")
        attempt += 1
if passwordValid:
    print("Password accepted")
else:
    print("Log on unsuccessful")
```

Regular expressions

A regular expression is a special sequence of characters which can be used to check that user input is in the correct "form" or "pattern". The Python module `re` provides support for regular expressions, and needs to be imported at the start of the program.

A list of some of the most common regular expressions is given below.

Expression	Description
[A-R]	Uppercase letter from A to R
[ADF]	Matches A, D or F
[A-Z]{3}	Exactly three uppercase letters from A to Z
[A-Z]{1,2}	One or two uppercase letters from A to Z
[0-9]{3,}	Three or more digits
[0-5]	Digit between 0 and 5
\d	Digit
[a-z]+	One or more lowercase characters
[a-z]*	Zero or more lowercase characters
[a-z]?	0 or 1 lowercase characters
\s	Space (e.g. [A-Z]\s\d{1,2} will find B 56 and B 1 valid, B52 and BN 3 invalid
A|B	A or B, where A and B are themselves regular expressions

Note that instead of writing \s to indicate a space in a regular expression, you can simply leave a space.

These expressions may be combined to perform a **format check** or to match complex combinations of letters and numbers, for example, different postcodes or car registration numbers.

6

Example 4

Use a regular expression to check that a user ID entered by the user consists of one or two uppercase letters followed by three digits.

```
#Program name: Ch 6 Example 4 regular expression1.py

#import regular expression module
import re

userID = input("Enter your user ID: ")
validID = re.match("[A-Z]{1,2}[0-9]{3}", userID)
if validID:
    print("Valid ID entered")
else:
    print("Invalid ID")
```

Example 5

A product code starts with one or two uppercase letters, followed by four or more digits, and ends with either H or G. Accept a number of product codes from the user and use a regular expression to validate them. The end of the data entry is signalled by entering the letter 'x'.

```
#Program name: Ch6 Example 5 regular expression2.py

#import regular expression module
import re

print("""A valid product code
starts with one or two uppercase letters,
followed by four or more digits,
and ends with either H or G""")
productCode = input("Enter a product code ('x' to end): ")
while productCode != "x":
    valid = re.match("[A-Z]{1,2}[0-9]{4,}[HG]", productCode)
    if valid:
        print("Valid product code entered")
    else:
        print("Invalid product code")
    productCode = input("Enter a product code ('x' to end): ")
```

Example 6

Use a regular expression to check that a password contains at least one digit.

```
#Program name: Ch6 Example 6 regular expression3.py
import re
password = input("Enter password: ")
validPassword = re.match("[a-zA-Z]*\d[a-zA-Z0-9]*", password)
if validPassword:
    print("Valid password")
else:
    print("Invalid password")
```

Exercises

1. A Dramatic Society wants to record the number of tickets sold for each of their four performances. Ask the user to enter the number of tickets sold for each performance. The number must be between 0 and 120. Print an error message if an invalid number is entered, and ask them to re-enter until they enter a valid number. Print the total number of tickets sold and the average attendance for a performance.

2. Write a program to ask the user to enter a car registration number, which must be in the format AANN AAA. Validate the entry and if invalid, ask the user to re-enter it.

3. Write a program to ask a user to enter their email address. They should then be asked to enter it again, and if it does not match the first entry, the user is asked to start over. Print a suitable message when the email address is correctly verified.

4. Write a program to ask a user to enter a new password. The password must be between 8 and 15 characters long and have at least one lowercase letter, one uppercase letter and one numeric character. If it does not, the user should repeatedly be asked to enter a different password until they enter a valid one.

5. Passwords on a file are to be stored in encrypted form so that they cannot easily be hacked by someone looking at the file.

    A simple "Caesar cipher" is used to encrypt a password by adding 3 to the ASCII value of each letter, converting this back to a character and storing the result. For example, the password BENXY3 would be stored as EHQAB6.

    Write a program to ask a user to enter a password. This is then encrypted and checked against the encrypted password held in the variable `storedPassword`. Assume, for test purposes, that the value held in `storedPassword` is EHQAB6.

    If the user enters an incorrect password, they are given two more attempts to get it right before being denied access.

Chapter 7
Searching and sorting

Objectives

- Use the dictionary data structure to look up data
- Sort a one-dimensional list in ascending or descending sequence
- Sort a two-dimensional list on a specified column

Dictionary data structure

You have used **strings**, **lists** and **tuples** in Chapters 4, 5 and 6. These are all known as **container** data types, because they can contain several items of data. There is another useful container data type called a **dictionary**.

A dictionary stores data items in pairs, with each pair consisting of a **key** and a **value**. It functions just like a printed dictionary, where you can look up a word (the key) and find its definition (the value).

Like a list, a dictionary is **mutable**, meaning that its values can be changed.

A dictionary is written in curly brackets, with each key value pair being separated by commas. In the statements written in the interactive Shell window shown below, the dictionary is called `studentMarks` and contains a number of student names and the mark they obtained in a test.

```
>>> studentMarks = {"Wesley":5, "Jo":9, "Betty":6, "Robina":5}
>>> studentMarks
{'Wesley': 5, 'Jo': 9, 'Betty': 6, 'Robina': 5}
>>> studentMarks["Betty"]
6
```

To look up the mark obtained by a particular student (the key), write the name of the dictionary followed by the key in square brackets. You cannot index a dictionary in the same way as a list, using an index number – an item can only be accessed through its key.

Q1 Write a statement to print the mark obtained by Robina.

Dictionary methods

The table below shows some of the most useful built-in dictionary methods.

Method	Description
get(key,[default])	Returns the value associated with key. If key is not in the dictionary, then the optional default is returned. If key is not in the dictionary and default is not specified then None is returned
keys()	Returns a view of all the keys in the dictionary
values()	Returns a view of all the values in the dictionary
items()	Returns a view of all the items. Each item in the dictionary is a two-element tuple , e.g. ("Wesley",5)

The interactive session below illustrates these methods.

```
>>> studentMarks = {"Wesley":5, "Jo":9, "Betty":6, "Robina":5}
>>> studentMarks.get("Betty","not found")
6
>>> studentMarks.get("Bill","not found")
'not found'
>>> studentMarks.keys()
dict_keys(['Wesley', 'Jo', 'Betty', 'Robina'])
>>> studentMarks.values()
dict_values([5, 9, 6, 5])
>>> studentMarks.items()
dict_items([('Wesley', 5), ('Jo', 9), ('Betty', 6), ('Robina', 5)])
```

Example 1a: Looking up a value

If you try to print the mark for a student whose name is not in the dictionary, Python will return an error. To avoid this, you should test whether the key is in the dictionary before trying to access it.

```
studentMarks = {"Wesley":5, "Jo":9, "Betty":6, "Robina":5}
name = input("Enter a student name to look up: ")
if name in studentMarks:
    print("Mark: ", studentMarks[name])
else:
    print("Name not found")
```

Example 1b: Adding a new key-value pair

Before adding a new key-value pair, you should check that the key is not already in the dictionary:

```
name = input("Enter a student name to add: ")
if name in studentMarks:
    print("Name is already in the marks record")
else:
    mark = input("Enter mark: ")
    studentMarks[name] = mark
```

Example 1c: Editing a value in an existing key:value pair

```
name = input("Enter a student name to edit their mark: ")
if name in studentMarks:
    mark = input("Enter mark: ")
    studentMarks[name] = mark
else:
    print("Name not found")
```

Example 1d: Deleting a key:value pair

```
name = input("Enter a student name to delete: ")
if name in studentMarks:
    del studentMarks[name]
else:
    print("Name not found")
```

Example 1e: Sorting a dictionary in order of keys

Python has a handy function called `sorted()` for sorting a dictionary by key value, shown in this interactive session:

```
>>> studentMarks = {"Wesley":5, "Jo":9, "Betty":6, "Robina":5}
>>> studentSorted = sorted(studentMarks.keys())
>>> studentSorted
['Betty', 'Jo', 'Robina', 'Wesley']
```

The code below prints all the student names and marks in key order:

```
for name in sorted(studentMarks.keys()):
    print(name, studentMarks[name])
```

The dictionary data structure is most useful for looking things up. For many other applications, a list is more flexible. A table of list operations was given in Chapter 5.

Storing a list in a dictionary

The value in the `key:value` pairs of a dictionary can itself be a tuple or list. For example, suppose you wanted to store a dictionary of anagrams, for example:

angel: angle, glean

trade: rated, tread

predator: parroted, teardrop

garden: danger, gander, ranged

The dictionary could be held like this:

```
anagrams =   {"angel": ("angle","glean"),
              "trade":("rated","tread"),
              "predator": ("parroted","teardrop"),
              "garden": ("danger","gander","ranged"),
              "berate": ("beater","rebate")}
```

Sorting a list

To sort a list, you can use the `sort()` method.

```
>>> alist = [6,2,8,4,0,2,33]
>>> alist.sort()
>>> alist
[0, 2, 2, 4, 6, 8, 33]
```

Example 2

The `sorted()` function can be used on lists and tuples as well as dictionaries, and provides an alternative way of sorting a list. To sort the original list `alist`, saving the new list in `blist`, you can write

```
blist = sorted(alist)
```

To print `alist` in sorted order, you could use a `for` loop:

```
for number in sorted(alist):
    print(number)
```

To sort `alist` in reverse order, write

```
blist = sorted(alist, reverse = True)
```

Sorting a two-dimensional list

As you saw in Chapter 5, a two-dimensional list can be envisaged as a table of values, with rows and columns.

7

	Column 0	Column 1	Column 2
	Surname	**Firstname**	**Exam mark**
Row 0	Harvey	Ron	56
Row 1	Jones	Alan	85
Row 2	Lansbury	Christine	68
Row 3	Mills	David	72

Table 1

In Python, such a table is held as a "list of lists", as shown in Example 3 below.

 Q2 "Ron" is contained in cell `studentMarks[0][1]`. Which cell contains "Lansbury"?

Example 3

A two-dimensional list `studentMarks` contains the values shown in Table 1. Write a program to sort and print the table in both ascending and descending order of exam mark.

The **lambda** keyword allows you to specify which element to sort on. It is used as shown below.

```
#Program name: Ch 7 Example 3 sort 2-D list.py
studentMarks = [ ["Harvey","Ron",56],
   ["Jones","Alan",85],
   ["Lansbury", "Christine", 68],
   ["Mills","David", 72] ]
#sort on column 2
studentMarksAscending = sorted(studentMarks,
   key=lambda x:x[2])
studentMarksDescending = sorted(studentMarks,
   key=lambda x:x[2], reverse = True)
print("Ascending order of mark")
for n in range(len(studentMarks)):
   print(studentMarksAscending[n])
print("\nDescending order of mark")
for n in range(len(studentMarks)):
   print(studentMarksDescending[n])
```

Q3 Amend the above program to sort the marks in ascending order of surname.

Exercises

1. Write a program in which a dictionary of anagrams is pre-defined. The program asks the user to enter a word, and then returns a list of all the anagrams of that word, or "Word not found" if the word is not in the dictionary. The user can continue to enter words until they enter "end" to quit.

2. Write a program which stores a dictionary of names and 2-digit telephone extensions. Display a menu of options from which the user can choose:

   A   Look up a telephone number

   B   Add a new name and telephone number

   C   Edit a telephone number

   D   Delete an entry

   E   Print phone directory in name sequence

   F   Quit

   Implement each of these choices.

3. Store the following data in a two-dimensional list. Print the data for the six months with the highest maximum temperatures, in descending order of maximum temperature.

Month	Max temp (°C)	Min temp (°C)
January	6	3
February	7	3
March	10	4
April	13	6
May	17	9
June	20	12
July	22	14
August	21	14
September	19	12
October	14	9
November	10	6
December	7	3

4. Using the data above, print a list of all months in which the minimum temperature fell below 9°C. Show the month name, maximum and minimum. Also print a list of months with a maximum temperature of 20°C or above.

Chapter 8

Functions

Objectives

- Write functions with and without parameters
- Pass values to functions through parameters
- Accept return values from functions
- Understand and use local and global variables
- Divide a program up into separate subroutines (functions)

Types of subroutine

A **subroutine** is a self-contained section of code that performs one specific task. As your programs become larger, using subroutines allows you to organise the program into smaller chunks that are easier to understand, debug and maintain.

A function is a type of subroutine – the only type available in Python. Some other programming languages define another type of subroutine called a **procedure**, but a Python function is flexible enough to do everything you need in the way of a subroutine.

Built-in functions

You have already used some **built-in functions** such as `ord()`, `chr()`, `len()`, `sorted()`, `input()` and `print()`. These functions are part of the Python language.

The examples below show that there are different ways of calling a function. For example, the function `ord()` returns the ASCII value of a character. In the interactive window, you can try out the various ways of calling a function.

```
>>> asciiValue = ord("f")
>>> asciiValue
102
```

In the above example, the first statement calls the function ord(), passing it a **parameter** "f", and assigns the value calculated by the function to a variable called asciiValue.

In the next example, the function ord() is called without explicitly assigning it to a variable, passing it the parameter "a".

```
>>> newValue = ord("a") + 3
>>> newChar = chr(newValue)
>>> print(newChar)
d
```

Notice that print() is itself a function, but the output from the function is not assigned to a variable. It is called by simply writing the name of the function with one or more parameters in parentheses. However, print() has some special syntax not available in an ordinary function.

 Q1 Write a statement which calls the input() function. Pass a parameter "Input your age:" to the function. Assign the value returned by the function to a variable called age.

Writing your own functions

- A programmer-written function starts with a statement giving the function name – a single line beginning with the word def, and ending with a colon.

- All the statements within the function are indented.

- A function is called by writing its name, in the same way you call an inbuilt function such as ord() or chr().

8

Example 1

Write a function which asks the user for their name and then prints "Hello, Jo" or whatever name the user enters.

```
#Program name: Ch 8 Example 1 print a greeting v1.py
#program to get name and print a greeting
def getAndPrintName():
    name = input("Please enter your name: ")
    print ("Hello",name)

#Main program
getAndPrintName()
```

The line

```
getAndPrintName()
```

is the **call** statement that tells the program to go and execute the function.

Note that the function itself must be placed above the statement which calls the function. When the Python compiler comes to the function definition, it does not execute it, but it makes a note that it is present, ready to be called. When the call statement is reached, it will know where to find the function and will then execute it. It may be called many times during the execution of the program.

Using parameters and return values

Just as with built-in functions, you can provide parameters for the function to use, and receive values back from the function. The function in Example 1 would probably be more useful if it could be used to print different messages, and return the name entered by the user so that it could be used in other circumstances or applications.

Example 2

In this example, the function prints a message specified as a parameter in the statement which calls the function. The name entered by the user is passed back to the variable called `playerName`, using a `return` statement.

```
#Program name: Ch 8 Example 2 print a greeting v2.py
def getAndPrintName(message):
    name = input("Please enter your name: ")
    print(message, name)
    return name

#main program
playerName = getAndPrintName("Hello")
print(playerName, "is Player 1")
```

Q2 What will be output by the above program?

Q3 Write a function called `birthday()` which accepts as parameters a name and age, and prints, for example: "Happy Birthday, Amy! You're 3 today!".

Using a docstring (documentation string)

You can document your functions with a special statement called a **docstring**. This is used in Example 3 on the next page. It can spread over as many lines as you like, enclosed in triple quotes at the head of a program or function.

Example 3

Write a function named `displayRules()` to display the rules of a game. Write a statement to call the function.

```
"""Program name: Ch 8 Example 3 using a docstring.py
Author: PG Online
Date written: 29/05/2017"""

def displayRules():
    """Display the game rules"""
    print("""
    The rules of the game are as follows:
    Players take turns to throw two dice.
    If the throw is a 'double', etc.
        """)

#call the function
displayRules()
```

In this example, there is no need to pass any parameters because the rules will always be the same. Nothing is returned from the function so there is no `return` statement.

Example 4

Here is an example of a program which uses a function to find the average of three numbers.

```
#Program name: Ch 8 Example 4 find average v1.py
def findAverage(x,y,z):
    total = x + y + z
    average = total/3
    return average

#main program
print("""This program uses a function
to find the average of 3 numbers \n""")
num1 = float(input("Enter first number: "))
num2 = float(input("Enter second number: "))
num3 = float(input("Enter third number: "))
result = findAverage(num1, num2, num3)
print("Average is ",result)
```

The parameters num1, num2 and num3 will be referred to as x, y and z in the function. The order in which you write the parameters in the statement which calls the function should be the same as the order in which they appear in the function heading.

8

Returning several values from a function

A function may return more than one value, as for example the function `userInput()` in Example 5 below. Note how the call statement is written in this case:

```
num1, num2, num3 = userInput()
```

Example 5

The program given in Example 4 could be further split up so that each part of it is performed by a function, and the main program is just a series of function calls. Of course, you would be unlikely to do this with such a trivial program, but the example below illustrates several points.

```python
#Program name: Ch 8 Example 5 find average v2.py
#program finds average of three numbers input by the user

def findAverage(x,y,z):
    total = x + y + z
    average = total/3
    return average

def printHeading():
    print("This program uses a function",
        "to find the average of 3 numbers\n")

def userInput():
    n1 = float(input("Enter first number: "))
    n2 = float(input("Enter second number: "))
    n3 = float(input("Enter third number: "))
    return n1, n2, n3

def printResult(answer):
    print("Average is ",answer)

#main program
printHeading()
num1, num2, num3 = userInput()
average = findAverage(num1, num2, num3)
printResult(average)
```

A note about procedures and functions

In programming languages which make a distinction between procedures and functions, the differences could be roughly summarised as follows:

- A **procedure** is a subroutine which performs a specific task, such as displaying the rules of a game. It may pass values back to the calling program, but it does this differently from a function. It is called simply by writing the name of the procedure with any parameters in parentheses. It may not have any parameters. In a different programming language, the first line might be something like:

```
procedure displayRules;
```

The procedure is called by simply writing its name:

```
displayRules;
```

- A **function** always returns one or more values that it has either calculated or that a user has input. It normally has at least one parameter and a `return` statement (or equivalent) to return the calculated value to the statement it was called from. In a different programming language, the first line might be something like:

```
function total(a,b,c);
```

The function is called using an assignment statement:

```
sum = total(a,b,c);
```

- In Python, both types of subroutine are referred to as **functions** and the first line is always written using the `def` keyword followed by the function name and any parameters in parentheses. For example:

```
def displayRules():
```

or

```
def total(a,b,c):
```

The call statement is written differently depending on whether or not the function returns one or more values, as shown in the following four examples:

```
displayRules()
sum = total(a,b,c)
average = total(a,b,c) / 3
maxMark, minMark = markStats(markList)
```

8

Local and global variables

The function `findAverage()` in Example 5 uses a variable called `total`. If you try to access `total` outside the subroutine, you will get a syntax error:

```
...line 26, in <module>
    print(total)
NameError: name 'total' is not defined
```

Local variables

In `findAverage()`, `total` is a **local variable**, known only in the function in which it is used. Using only local variables in a function keeps it self-contained and means it can be used in many different programs without the programmer having to worry about what variable names have been used. You could have three functions all containing a local variable called `total` and they could hold three completely different values.

Example 6

The following program illustrates the use of local variables.

```python
#Program name: Ch 8 Example 6 local variables.py
#program to illustrate use of local variables

def nameOne():
    myName = "Alice"
    print("In function nameOne, name = ", myName)

def nameTwo():
    myName = "Bob"
    print("In function nameTwo, name = ", myName)

#main program
myName = "Kumar"
print("In main program, name = ", myName)
nameOne()
print("In main program, name = ", myName)
nameTwo()
print("In main program, name = ", myName)
```

In each of the functions `nameOne()` and `nameTwo()`, the variable `myName` is a local variable and completely separate from any variable with the same identifier used elsewhere in the program. This implements the important principle of **encapsulation**, whereby a subroutine encapsulates or holds all the variables it needs to execute and so can be used in any program without any danger of conflicting variable names.

8

The output from this program is:

```
In main program, name =  Kumar
In function nameOne, name =  Alice
In main program, name =  Kumar
In function nameTwo, name =  Bob
In main program, name =  Kumar
```

Global variables

A **global variable** can be used anywhere in a program, including within any functions called.

Example 7

```
#Program name: Ch 8 Example 7 local and global variables.py
#program to illustrate use of local and global variables

def nameOne():
    global myName
    print("In function nameOne, name = ", myName)
    myName = "Alice"
    print("In function nameOne, name = ", myName)

def nameTwo():
    myName = "Bob"
    print("In function nameTwo, name = ", myName)

#main program
myName = "Kumar"
print("In main program, name = ", myName)
nameOne()
print("In main program, name = ", myName)
nameTwo()
print("In main program, name = ", myName)
```

To use myName (defined in the main program) in function nameOne, for example, without passing it as a parameter, you must define it as a global variable in the function.

In function nameOne (), the variable myName has been defined as a global variable, so it is the same variable, held in the same memory location, as myName defined in the main program. When it is changed in the function, it is also changed in the main program and its new value is printed in the main program.

The output from this program is:

```
In main program, name =  Kumar
In function nameOne, name =  Kumar
In function nameOne, name =  Alice
In main program, name =  Alice
In function nameTwo, name =  Bob
In main program, name =  Alice
```

You should generally avoid using global variables, as it can be hard to keep track of their values. Their use can cause hard-to-detect errors and make a program difficult to maintain.

Remember that functions should be self-contained, so that the same function can be used in many different programs without the programmer having to worry about whether variable names used in their program will conflict with a variable name used in the function. Any values needed in the function should be passed as parameters.

> **Q4** What will be the output if you insert an extra line
>
> ```
> global myName
> ```
>
> in function `nameTwo()`?

Exercises

1. Write program to accept a value, representing the side of a cube, from the user and call a function to return the surface area and volume of the cube. Display the results.

2. Write a program which asks the user to enter a short message. Call a function to encrypt the message by rearranging the letters in the sequence 2,4,6,...1,3,5...

    For example, `"Hello Jo"` will be encrypted as `el oHloJ`.

    Print the encoded message.

3. Write a program which asks the users to enter the average temperature for seven days of a week. Call a function which finds and returns the maximum average temperature and the day on which it occurred.

4. Write a program which asks the user to enter an employee name, hourly pay rate and the hours worked on each day of the week. Call a function to calculate total pay for the week, assuming time and a half on Saturdays and double time on Sundays.

    Display the employee name, total hours worked and total pay.

Chapter 9
Reading and writing files

Objectives

- Read from a text file
- Open a new file and write data to it
- Append data to an existing file
- Interrogate and process data stored in a file
- Use format operators and modifiers to format output

Storing data

When a user runs a program which asks them to type in data, the data is held in memory (RAM), and unless it is transferred to a permanent storage medium, it will be lost as soon as the program ends.

This chapter describes how to store data in a **text file** on a hard disk or other storage device so that it can be retrieved later for processing.

There are several ways of creating a text file. We can use a program to ask the user to enter the data, and store it after each record has been entered. We can download data from a website and then save it in a file.

One very simple way of creating a text file is to use a text editor such as Notepad. The first exercise shows how, in a Python program, you can read a file created in this way.

Records and fields

There is a file called **films.txt** on the website **www.pgonline.co.uk** which you can download. Alternatively, you can use a text editor to type the first few records from the file and save it as **films.txt** in the same folder as your programs.

```
001,Ghostbusters,2016,PG,116,Comedy
002,The Legend of Tarzan,2016,PG,109,Action
003,Jason Bourne,2016,PG,123,Action
004,The Nice Guys,2016,R,116,Crime
005,The Secret Life of Pets,2016,G,91,Animation
006,Star Trek Beyond,2016,PG,120,Action
etc…
```

Each record in the file is typed on a new line, so ten records are shown above. The end of a record is signified by a **newline character, \n**. You will not see the newline character when you print a string, but you will see its effect, which is to move to the next line before printing.

Each record is split into **fields**, separated usually by commas or optionally, another separator. There are six fields in each of the records shown, and in the text file, all the fields are string fields. It will be up to the programmer to separate the fields and convert them to the appropriate field type for processing.

Note: In this file, the invisible newline character \n is the last character of the sixth field, genre.

The table below is a description of each of the fields in the file:

Field name	Field type	Description
filmID	string	Unique identifier
title	string	Film title
yearReleased	integer	Year of release
rating	string	Classification; must be G, PG or R
duration	integer	Duration of film in minutes
genre	string	Must be Action, Animation, Fantasy, Comedy or Crime

In the real world films are rated differently in different countries and there are more than three classifications. There are also many more genres of film, but for this purpose we will keep things simple.

Opening, reading and closing a text file

Before a file can be read or written to, it must be opened. The `open` statement assigns a variable name to the file, tells the program where the file is located, what its name is and in what **mode** it is to be opened (**read**, **write** or **append**).

To assign the variable name `myFile` to a text file named `films.txt` held in the same folder as the Python program and open it for reading:

```
myFile = open("films.txt", "r")
```

Example 1

Open the file named **films.txt**, held in the same folder as the Python program, read all the records and print them out.

```
#Program name: Ch 9 Example 1 read film file.py
filmFile = open("films.txt","r")
films = filmFile.read()
print(films)
filmFile.close()
```

In the `open` statement, `"r"` stands for **read mode**. When opened in this mode it is not possible to change a record or write a new record to the file.

Note that the film file should be closed before exiting the program.

The program in Example 1 will print all the records in the file, but you cannot access individual records. To do that, you need to read the file one line at a time. You can then split each record into its individual fields ready for processing.

In Example 2 below, the statement `filmRec = filmFile.readline()` is performed once before entry into the `while` loop, and again at the end of the loop. The end of file is detected when an empty record is read.

The first statement in the `while` loop specifies that a comma has been used as the separator, and splits the record that has just been read into individual indexed strings referred to as `field[0]`, `field[1]` etc.

Example 2

Read each record in the **films.txt** file and split it into individual fields. Print the ID, title, rating and duration of all the films having a rating "G".

```
#Program name: Ch 9 Example 2 films rated G.py
filmFile = open("films.txt","r")
filmRec = filmFile.readline()
while filmRec != "":
    field = filmRec.split(",")
    ID = field[0]
    title = field[1]
    rating = field[3]
    duration = int(field[4])
    genre = field[5]
    if rating == "G":
        print(ID,title,rating,duration)
    filmRec = filmFile.readline()
filmFile.close()
```

9

The output looks like this:

```
005 The Secret Life of Pets G 91
008 Finding Dory G 103
009 Zootopia G 108
026 The Good Dinosaur G 101
```

This works fine, but something odd happens if you try to print out all films with a genre of Comedy. Nothing is printed, even though the file contains five records of that genre!

The reason is that genre is the last field in each record, and so contains the invisible \n character at the end of the field. Therefore you need to include that character in the string you are searching for.

Example 3

Read each record in the **films.txt** file and split it into individual fields. Print the ID, title, rating and genre and duration of all the films having genre Comedy.

```
#Program name: Ch 9 Example 3 comedy films v1.py
filmFile = open("films.txt","r")
filmRec = filmFile.readline()
while filmRec != "":
    field = filmRec.split(",")
    ID = field[0]
    title = field[1]
    rating = field[3]
    duration = int(field[4])
    genre = field[5]
    if genre == "Comedy\n":
        print(ID,title,rating,genre,duration)
    filmRec = filmFile.readline()
filmFile.close()
```

This will print:

```
001 Ghostbusters PG Comedy
 116
022 The Intern PG Comedy
 121
023 Ted 2 R Comedy
 121
024 Trainwreck R Comedy
 122
029 Birdman R Comedy
 119
```

Notice that the newline character has caused the `duration` field to be printed on the next line. In Example 5 we will slice off the newline character to prevent this from happening.

Using a `for` loop to read a file line-by-line

You can use a `for` loop to read each line of a file and print it. Remember that the last field ends with the newline character \n, and although the character will not be printed it will cause a move to the next line. Since each print statement also causes a move to the next line, your printout will be double spaced. If you do not want this to happen, you can end each print statement with `end = " "` to prevent the next print statement from automatically inserting its own newline character.

Example 4

Use a `for` loop to read and print each line of the file.

```
#Program name: Ch 9 Example 4 read and print each film record.py

filmFile = open("films.txt","r")
for row in filmFile:
    field = row.split(",")
    print(field[0],
    field[1],field[2],field[3],field[4],field[5],end ="")
filmFile.close()
```

The next example has the same requirements as Example 3, but this time we will delete the newline character using Python's **slicing** so that the printout appears correctly.

Example 5

Read each record in the **films.txt** file and split it into individual fields. Print the ID, title, yearReleased, rating, genre and duration of all the films having genre `Comedy`.

```
#Program name: Ch 9 Example 5 comedy films.py
filmFile = open("films.txt","r")
for row in filmFile:
    field = row.split(",")
    ID = field[0]
    title = field[1]
    yearReleased = field[2]
    rating = field[3]
    duration = int(field[4])
    genre = field[5]
```

9

```
#slice off the last character of genre, which is "\n"
   lastchar = len(genre)- 1
   genre = genre[0:lastchar]
   if genre == "Comedy":
      print(ID,title,yearReleased,rating,genre,duration)
filmFile.close()
```

This prints:

```
001 Ghostbusters 2016 PG Comedy 116
022 The Intern 2015 PG Comedy 121
023 Ted 2 2015 R Comedy 121
024 Trainwreck 2015 R Comedy 122
029 Birdman 2014 R Comedy 119
```

Writing to a file

New records can be written to a file by opening it in **write mode**:

```
filmFile = open("films.txt","w")
```

This will create a new file. If a file named films.txt already exists, it will be overwritten.

Alternatively, you can open a file in **append mode:**

```
filmFile = open("films.txt","a")
```

This will create a new file if none exists, or open an existing file after the last record.

In the next example, a file is created to hold data showing the local time and the temperature in °C of several cities around the world on a particular day in February, when it is midday in London.

The sample data to be entered is:

City	Temperature	Local time
London	7	1200
Accra	30	1200
Baghdad	20	1500
Winnipeg	-12	0600
New York	14	0700
Nairobi	27	1500
Sydney	22	2300

This time, the newline character \n will be held as a separate field at the end of each record and not simply appended to the last field of the record.

Example 6

Write a program to create a new file called **temperatures.txt**, or append records to the file if one already exits.

```
#Program name: Ch 9 Example 6 append to temperatures file.py
tempsFile= open("temperatures.txt", "a")
print("This program writes temperature data to \n
temperatures.txt")
print("If the file does not exist, it will be created")
city = input("Enter city name, xxx to end: ")

while city != "xxx":
    temperature = input("Enter temperature: ")
    localTime = input("Enter local time: ")
    tempsFile.write(city + "," + temperature + "," + localTime
    + "," + "\n")
    city = input("Enter city name, xxx to end: ")

#endwhile
filmFile.close()
```

The user signals the end of input by entering xxx.

Note that each field is separated by a comma, and a newline character is added to the end of each line to signal the end of the record.

(a) Write a program to read and print all the records in **temperatures.txt**.

(b) Open the file **temperatures.txt** in Notepad. Note the commas at the end of each line, indicating that the invisible newline character is in a field of its own.

File processing

Often, data held in a file will need to be processed in some way, as shown in Example 7 overleaf. Remember that all data in a text file are held as strings, so that if any calculations are to be done, the relevant data field must first be converted to an integer or floating point number using int() or float().

If any calculated data is to be written back to a second text file, it must first be converted to a string using the str() function.

In Example 7 below, data is read from the text file **temperatures.txt** into a two-dimensional list, (i.e. a table or a list of sublists), with each sublist containing the data from one row in the text file plus the calculated Fahrenheit temperature.

The rows are then sorted in descending order on the `temperatureC` field. Each row is then printed.

You can visualise this two-dimensional list as a table:

	Column 0 (city)	Column 1 (temp C)	Column 2 (temp F)	Column 3 (local time)
Row 0	London	7	44.6	1200
Row 1	Accra	30	86.0	1200
Row 2	Baghdad	20	68.0	1500
etc	...	...	....	...

The following steps are carried out:

```
for each row in the text file
    Read a row into cityRec
    Split cityRec into individual fields
    Convert the temperature field to a floating point number (or
    an integer)
    Convert the temperature to Fahrenheit
    Append the individual fields to the list newCityRec[] - this
    is one row in the table
    Append the list newCityRec to the table cityTable
    Clear newCityRec ready to receive the data from the next row
    in the table
endfor
Sort the list on column 1, temperatureC

for each row in the table
    print individual fields
endfor
```

Example 7

Read the data in the file **temperatures.txt**, convert all the Centigrade temperatures to Fahrenheit, sort the data in descending order of temperature and print it out giving both the Centigrade and Fahrenheit temperatures.

```
#Program name: Ch 9 Example 7 process temperatures file.py
tempsFile = open("temperatures.txt", "r")
cityTable = []
newCityRec = []
```

```
for row in tempsFile:
    cityRec = row.split(",")
    city = cityRec[0]
    temperatureC = float(cityRec[1])
    tempF = (temperatureC * 9/5) + 32
    localTime = cityRec[2]

    newCityRec.append(city)
    newCityRec.append(temperatureC)
    newCityRec.append(tempF)
    newCityRec.append(localTime)

    #Append record to table, and clear newCityRec for next record
    cityTable.append(newCityRec)
    newCityRec = []

#All the records are now held in a 2-D list called cityTable
#Sort the list in descending sequence on temperatureC
#Refer to Chapter 7 for how to do this using the lambda function

sortedTable = sorted(cityTable, key=lambda x:x[1], reverse=True)
print("\nList of cities in descending order of temperature \n")
for n in range (len(sortedTable)):
    print(sortedTable[n][0],sortedTable[n][1], sortedTable[n][2],
    sortedTable[n][3])
tempsFile.close()
```

This produces the following output:

```
List of cities in descending order of temperature

Accra 30.0 86.0 1200
Nairobi 27.0 80.6 1500
Sydney 22.0 71.6 2300
Baghdad 20.0 68.0 1500
New York 14.0 57.2 0700
London 7.0 44.6 1200
Winnipeg -12.0 10.399999999999999 0600
```

Q2 Suggest amendments to the above program so that both Centigrade and Fahrenheit temperatures are displayed to the nearest whole number.

9

Formatting output

The data printed above would look much better printed neatly in columns, with column headings at the top.

Format operators

To do this, Python provides **format operators** which are used to produce **formatted strings**.

The **%** operator is a string operator called the **format operator**. Using the format operator, instead of writing something like

```
print(city, temperatureC, localTime)
```

the statement is written as

```
print("%s,%d,%s" % (city, temperatureC, localTime))
```

We can try this out in IDLE to see what the output looks like:

```
>>> city = "London"
>>> temperatureC = 7
>>> localTime = "1200"
>>> print("%s,%d,%s" % (city, temperatureC, localTime))
London,7,1200
>>> print("The temperature in %s was %d degrees C at %s"
    % (city,temperatureC,localTime))
The temperature in London was 7 degrees C at 1200
```

The formatting expression is divided into two parts.

The first part, `"%s,%d,%s"`, contains one or more format specifications. A conversion character tells the format operator what type of value is to be inserted into that position in the string; `%s` indicates a string, `%d` indicates an integer.

The second part, `% (city, temperatureC, localTime)`, specifies the values that are to be printed.

> **Q3** Write statements to do the following:
>
> set a = 3, b = 4, c = a + b, d = a * b.
>
> Use format operators to print the statements:
>
> ```
> 3 + 4 = 7
> The product of 3 and 4 is 12
> ```

Format modifiers

Format modifiers can be used to:

- specify a field width
- specify the number of digits after the decimal point
- left- or right-justify a value with a specified field width

Table 9.1 shows the more common formatting conversion characters, and Table 9.2 shows the format modifiers.

Character	Output format
d	Integer
f	Floating point as dd.ddddd
c	Single character
s	String, or any Python object that can be converted to a string using str()
%	Insert a literal % character

Table 9.1: String formatting conversion characters

Character	Example	Description
number	%15s	Puts the value in a field of width 15 characters
-	%-15d	Puts the value in a field of width 15 characters, left-justified
+	%+15d	Puts the value in a field of width 15 characters, right-justified
0	%04d	Puts the value in a field of width four characters, filled with leading zeros
.	%15.2f	Puts the value in a field of width 15 characters, with two digits to the right of the decimal point

Table 9.2: Formatting options

Example 8

Rewrite the print statements from Example 7 so that the data is printed in neat tabular format.

```
print("%-20s%20s%20s%20s"
%("City","Temperature(C)","Temperature(F)","Local time"))
for n in range (len(sortedTable)):
    print ("%-20s%20.1f%20.1f%20s"
    %(sortedTable[n][0],sortedTable[n][1],sortedTable[n][2],
    sortedTable[n][3]))
```

This prints the data in the following format:

```
City              Temperature(C)      Temperature(F)      Local time
Accra                       30.0                86.0            1200
Nairobi                     27.0                80.6            1500
Sydney                      22.0                71.6            2300
Baghdad                     20.0                68.0            1500
New York                    14.0                57.2            0700
London                       7.0                44.6            1200
Winnipeg                   -12.0                10.4            0600
```

Exercises

1. Write a program to write or append records to a file named `students.txt` containing student details.

   To keep things simple, you are advised to ensure that the newline character occupies a field of its own, using the technique shown in Example 6 on page 65.

   Each record will have the following fields:

   ```
   Username, firstname, surname, gender, year
   ```

   Add several records to the file.

2. Open `students.txt` in read mode and print the names of all the girls in Year 10. Format the output so that it appears in columns under appropriate headings, surname followed by first name.

3. Print the surname, first name, gender and year of all the students in `students.txt` in ascending order of surname, formatted in columns.

4. Open `students.txt` in Notepad. There should be a comma at the end of each line, indicating that the newline character \n is separated from the last data field in each record, and occupies its own field.

   Now open `films.txt` in Notepad. This file was created in Notepad, without adding an extra comma at the end of each line. This means that the last field in each record ends with the invisible newline character. For example,

   ```
   001,Ghostbusters,2016,PG,116,Comedy
   ```

   is held internally as

   ```
   001,Ghostbusters,2016,PG,116,Comedy\n
   ```

   and so in order to process the file, the last character must be stripped off as shown in Example 5 on pages 63-64. (\n is held as one character, not two, by the computer.)

   If you create a text file in Notepad, add a comma to the end of each line.

Chapter 10
Databases and SQL

Objectives

- Learn how data is held in a database so that information can be easily added, deleted, amended and retrieved
- Learn some database terms: table, record, field, primary key
- Write SQL statements to create a database table and add, update or delete data in the table
- Write SQL statements to query a database

Flat file databases

A database is a collection of records held in a number of different tables. In this book we will be concerned only with **flat file databases**, which contain just one table.

Within a database table, data is held in rows, with each row holding information about one person or thing. The data about city temperatures that we held in a text file in the last chapter could be held in a database table like this:

city	temperature	localTime
London	7	1200
Accra	30	1200
Baghdad	20	1500
Winnipeg	-12	0600
New York	14	0700
Nairobi	27	1500
Sydney	22	2300

Records, fields and primary keys

- A **record** is a row in a database table
- A **field** (also called an **attribute**) is held in a column in a database table

There are seven records, each with three fields, in the table shown on the previous page.

One of the fields is a special field known as an **identifier** or **primary key**, and this field uniquely identifies the record. In the table above, `city` is the primary key. The table cannot hold two records for the same city.

Using SQL

SQL (Structured Query Language) is a programming language that you can use to create, update and query a database. The version that you will be using with your Python programs is called SQLite.

Data types

When the database table, which we will call `tblTemps`, is created, the programmer must specify what type of data is held in each field.

Data types that you will use include `TEXT`, `INTEGER` and `REAL`. These can be written in either upper or lower case.

Data type	Description
TEXT	A text string of any length
INTEGER	A signed integer, e.g. -76, 0, 365
REAL	A floating point value, e.g. -3.7, 0.0, 56.458

Creating an empty table

The SQL command to create the empty table `tblTemps` is shown below:

```
CREATE TABLE tblTemps
(
city TEXT,
temperature INTEGER,
localTime TEXT,
primary key (city)
)
```

Note: Do not try typing this directly into Python – it won't work! In the next chapter, you will learn how to put SQL statements into a Python program.

Querying a database

The most useful thing about holding data in a database is how easy it is to query the database. The syntax for a `SELECT ... FROM ... WHERE` query is

SELECT	*list the fields to be displayed*
FROM	*specify the table where the data will come from*
WHERE	*list the search criteria*
ORDER BY	*list the fields that the results are to be sorted on (default is Ascending)*

For example, if you wanted to display the temperature and local time in Sydney (according to the simplified data held in our database), you would write

```
SELECT temperature, localTime
FROM tblTemps
WHERE city = "Sydney"
```

To display all the fields in each row of the table in alphabetical order of city, you would write

```
SELECT *
FROM tblTemps
ORDER BY city
```

To display just the first five records in descending order of temperature, write

```
SELECT *
FROM tblTemps
ORDER BY temperature DESC
LIMIT 5
```

Adding a record to a database table

To add a new record to an existing database table, use an `INSERT` query.

The syntax of this statement is:

```
INSERT INTO table_name(column1, column2, column3, ... columnN)
VALUES(value1, value2, value3, ... valueN)
```

If you are going to enter values into every field, you do not need to specify the columns. For example,

```
INSERT INTO tblTemps
VALUES("Montreal", -2, "0700")
```

If you wanted to enter a new record for a city but did not yet know the temperature at a particular time, you would write

```
INSERT INTO tblTemps(city, localTime)
VALUES("Brasilia", "0900")
```

10

Updating a record

To update a record, use the syntax

```
UPDATE table_name
SET column1 = value1, column2 = value2, … column = valueN)
WHERE [condition]
```

For example, to set the temperature in Brasilia to 20, write

```
UPDATE tblTemps
SET temperature = 20
WHERE city = "Brasilia"
```

You can combine several conditions using the AND or OR operators.

Deleting records from a table

The syntax of the DELETE statement is

```
DELETE FROM table_name
WHERE [condition]
```

For example, to delete all records which have temperatures below 10 and the local time is 1200, you would write:

```
DELETE FROM tblTemps
WHERE temperature < 10 AND localTime = "1200"
```

To delete all the records from the table, you would write

```
DELETE FROM tblTemps
```

In the next chapter, you will learn how to incorporate these SQL statements into a Python program.

10

Exercises

An online computer game asks players to log on before they play the game. It saves their first name, surname and player ID in a database. The database has one table called `tblScores`, which holds data in the following format:

Field name	Data type	Description
playerID	TEXT	Text string, 5 characters consisting of player's initials followed by 3 digits
firstname	TEXT	A text string of any length
surname	TEXT	A text string of any length
score1	INTEGER	Highest score achieved
score2	INTEGER	Second-highest score
score3	INTEGER	Third-highest score

1. Write an SQL statement to create the table `tblScores`.

2. Write an SQL statement to append a new record for Maria Ferdinand, player MF123, all scores set to zero.

3. Write an SQL statement to set `score1 = 87`, `score2 = 79` and `score3 = 63` in the record for Maria Ferdinand.

4. Write an SQL statement to query the database to find the highest score achieved by Maria Ferdinand.

5. Write an SQL statement to find all the data for Maria Ferdinand.

10

Chapter 11
Python's SQLite module

Objectives

- Import the SQLite library into a Python program
- Use SQL commands in a Python program to create a database and a database table
- Use SQL commands to query a database and print the results of the query
- Use SQL commands to add, amend and delete records in a table
- Use a `try` … `except` statement to trap user input errors

Using SQL commands in a Python program

There are several database packages that can be imported and used in a Python program, including MySQL, Sybase and SQLite. **SQLite** is a simple relational database system that is supplied with Python and can be imported into any Python program.

Creating a database

The first thing to do is to create a new database, and within the database, create a table to hold the data.

In Chapter 9 a text file called `films.txt`, holding data about films, was used. We will use the same data, this time storing it in a database table from where it can easily be queried, and have records added, updated or deleted.

First of all, the module `sqlite` needs to be imported.

To use a database, a **connection object** to represent the database has to be created using the SQLite connect method. The argument of the `connect` method is the name of the file, which is assumed in this example to be in the same folder as the program. If a file with this name does not exist in the folder, a new file will be created.

Here are the Python statements for these two steps:

```python
import sqlite3
connection = sqlite3.connect("MyFilms.db")
```

Note that `connection` is just a name chosen in this example – you could call it anything, for example `conn` or `c`.

This creates an empty database. The next thing to do is to create a table within the database.

The SQL syntax for doing this is:

```sql
CREATE TABLE tblFilms
(
    filmID TEXT,
    title TEXT,
    yearReleased INTEGER,
    rating TEXT,
    duration INTEGER,
    genre TEXT,
    primary key (filmID)
)
```

However, we want to do this from within the Python program, so we cannot simply write SQL statements, which Python will not understand.

In order to send an SQL statement to SQLite, a **cursor object** is required. This is a control structure used for performing all SQL commands. The following statement gets the cursor object assigned here, to a variable named `cursor`:

```python
cursor = connection.cursor
```

The SQL command is then written within triple quotes, and assigned to a variable. In the example below the variable name `sqlCommand` is used, but it could be anything.

The `commit()` method is needed to save the changes to the database.

Finally, you should close the connection with the statement `connection.close()`

The complete code for creating the database and the table is given below.

Example 1

```python
#Program name: Ch 11 Example 1 create films database.py
import sqlite3

#create or open a database called MyFilms.db
connection = sqlite3.connect("MyFilms.db")
cursor = connection.cursor()
```

```
#SQL to create the table structure of tblFilms in MyFilms.db

sqlCommand = """
   CREATE TABLE tblFilms
   (
   filmID TEXT,
   title TEXT,
   yearReleased INTEGER,
   rating TEXT,
   duration INTEGER,
   genre TEXT,
   primary key (filmID)
   ) """

cursor.execute(sqlCommand)
print("tblFilms created in MyFilms.db")

#The commit statement saves the changes to the database
connection.commit()
connection.close()
```

SQLite will accept either `STRING` or `TEXT` as a data type, in upper or lower case.

*Note: You can only run this program once, since it creates the database and the table within it. If you want to make some changes and run it again, you must first delete the database **MyFilms.db** from your folder.*

A second version of this program in the folder named `Ch 11 Example 1 create films database v2.py` calls a function `createTable()` to create the database table in a database called `MyFilms2.db`.

Importing data from a text file

We could enter the film data again from scratch, but since we already have it in a text file, we can just transfer it to the database table.

Example 2

Transfer data from a text file into a database, in which a new table has already been created.

The Python program shown below has a short main program which opens the text file. It then calls a function `readTextFile()`, passing the name of the text file as a parameter.

Within the function `readTextFile()`, a connection object is created and the cursor object is defined.

Each row in the database table will hold one row from the text file, split into its individual fields.

An empty list is assigned to `filmDBRec`, which will be loaded with the fields from the next line in the text file, ready to be transferred to the next record in the table `tblFilms`.

A `cursor.execute()` method is used to specify the SQL command to write the record to the database table. The `connection.commit()` method saves the changes to the database.

The list `filmDBRec` is then emptied and the process repeated in a `while` loop until all the records in the text file have been transferred.

```
#Program name: Ch 11 Example 2 transfer film records.py
#transfer records to film database from text file
import sqlite3

#function to read text records and store in record filmDBRec[]
def readTextFile(filmFile):
    connection = sqlite3.connect("MyFilms.db")
    cursor = connection.cursor()

    numRecs = 0
    filmDBRec = []
    filmTextRec = filmFile.readline()
    while filmTextRec != "":
        numRecs += 1
        field = filmTextRec.split(",")
        ID = field[0]
        title = field[1]
        yearReleased = field[2]
        rating = field[3]
        duration = int(field[4])
        genre = field[5]
        #strip off the newline character \n from genre
        lastchar = len(genre)- 1
        genre = genre[0:lastchar]
        print(ID, title,yearReleased,rating,duration,genre)

        #append fields to the list variable filmDBRec
        #to construct the record to be inserted
        filmDBRec.append(ID)
        filmDBRec.append(title)
        filmDBRec.append(yearReleased)
        filmDBRec.append(rating)
        filmDBRec.append(duration)
        filmDBRec.append(genre)
```

```
        #insert this record into the database
        cursor.execute ("INSERT INTO tblFilms VALUES (?,?,?,?,?,?)",
        filmDBRec)
        connection.commit()

        #empty the list of fields ready for next record
        filmDBRec = []
        #read the next record from the text file
        filmTextRec = filmFile.readline()
        #endwhile
    connection.close()
    return numRecs
    #end function readTextFile

#main
filmFile = open("films.txt","r")
numRecs = readTextFile(filmFile)
print("\n",numRecs,"records transferred")
#close the text file
filmFile.close()
```

A count is kept in the function `readTextFile()` of the number of records transferred, and this is returned and printed in the main program.

Creating a new database and loading it with data

11

There are several ways of getting data into a database table. We have seen in Example 2 how you can transfer data from a text file. In the next example, a new database is defined which will hold the temperature in different cities at a given time, in a table called **tblTemps**. This will use the same data used in Chapter 10.

The cursor's `executemany()` command is used to add multiple records.

Example 3

Create a new database named **CityTemperatures.db**, and within this database, a table named **tblTemps**. Define a list of tuples, each of which holds the data for one record. Use an SQL command to insert records into the table.

```
#Program name: Ch 11 Example 3 populate tblTemps.py
#Creates a table called tblTemps in database CityTemperatures.db
#then adds temperatures for several cities to tblTemps
import sqlite3

conn = sqlite3.connect("CityTemperatures.db")
cursor = conn.cursor()
```

```
#create a table
cursor.execute("""CREATE TABLE tblTemps
                (city TEXT,
                temperature INTEGER,
                localTime TEXT,
                primary key (city))
                """)

#insert multiple records
tblTemps =    [('London',7,'1200'),
              ('Accra',30,'1200'),
              ('Baghdad',20,'1500'),
              ('Winnipeg',-12,'0600'),
              ('New York',14,'0700'),
              ('Nairobi',27,'1500'),
              ('Sydney',22,'2300')
              ]
cursor.executemany("INSERT INTO tblTemps VALUES (?,?,?)",
tblTemps)

#save data to database
conn.commit()
conn.close()
print("Table successfully created")
```

An alternative program in the folder called Ch 11 Example 3 alternative solution.py, uses a function and a different way of writing the `connect()` statement to create a database called **CityTemperatures2.db**, containing an empty table **tblTemperatures**.

Querying the database

To make a query and print the results, use normal SQL syntax to define the query and then write a statement to make the cursor object execute the SQL.

The first example shows how to print all the records in the **CityTemperatures** database.

Example 4

```
#Program name: Ch 11 Example 4 print tblTemps.py
import sqlite3

conn = sqlite3.connect("CityTemperatures.db")
cursor = conn.cursor()
for row in cursor.execute
('SELECT * FROM tblTemps ORDER BY temperature DESC'):
   print (row)
```

The output is as follows:

```
('Accra', 30, '1200')
('Nairobi', 27, '1500')
('Sydney', 22, '2300')
etc.
```

The program in the folder also shows how to produce formatted output.

Example 5

You can specify how many records you want to output using the `LIMIT` parameter.

As with a text file, you can format the output neatly in columns: (See Tables 9.1, 9.2.)

```
#Program name: Ch 11 Example 5 print 5 recs in tblTemps.py
import sqlite3


conn = sqlite3.connect("CityTemperatures.db")
cursor = conn.cursor()
#print headings
print("%-15s%20s%20s" %("City","Temperature","Local time"))
for row in cursor.execute
('SELECT * FROM tblTemps ORDER BY temperature DESC LIMIT 5'):
    city, temperature, localTime = row
        print ("%-15s %15d %20s" %(city, temperature, localTime))
```

This produces output

```
City              Temperature        Local time
Accra                      30              1200
Nairobi                    27              1500
Sydney                     22              2300
Baghdad                    20              1500
New York                   14              0700
```

Example 6

You can specify a condition to determine which records will be printed. For example, you could print only records of cities with temperatures of 25 or more.

```
#Program name: Ch 11 Example 6 print temps 25 or more.py
import sqlite3


conn = sqlite3.connect("CityTemperatures.db")
cursor = conn.cursor()
```

```
sql = """
SELECT city, temperature
FROM tblTemps
WHERE temperature >= 25
ORDER BY temperature DESC
"""
for row in cursor.execute(sql):
    city, temperature = row
    print(row)
```

Adding records entered by the user

Often, a user will need to add, amend or delete a record from the database.

Example 7

Write a program to allow the user to add several records to `tblTemps`.

- In the first three lines of code, the `sqlite` module is imported, and a connection object and a cursor object are created, as before.

- An empty list `myRec[]` is created, which will be filled with the data to be entered into one row of the table. The first city name is entered.

- The `while` loop is entered, allowing the user to enter data which is appended to `myRec[]`.

- The record is inserted using the `cursor.execute()` method, and the `commit()` statement updates the database. `myRec[]` is emptied ready to hold the next record, and the user enters the next city name.

- The loop continues until the user enters `xxx` instead of a city name.

- The connection is closed.

```
#Program name: Ch 11 Example 7 add records to tblTemps.py
import sqlite3
conn = sqlite3.connect("CityTemperatures.db")
cursor = conn.cursor()

myRec = []
city = input("\nEnter city name: ")
while city != "xxx":
    temperature = int(input ("Enter temperature: "))
    localTime = input ("Enter local time: ")
    myRec.append(city)
    myRec.append(temperature)
    myRec.append(localTime)
```

```
        cursor.execute("INSERT INTO tblTemps VALUES (?,?,?)", myRec)
        conn.commit()
        myRec = []
        city = input("\nEnter city name (xxx to end): ")
    conn.close()
```

Trapping errors

If the user enters the name of a city which is already in the database, the program will crash, because `city` is a key field. A key field has to be unique in a database table.

Example 8

In order to prevent this happening, you can include a `try ... except` clause. In the code above, replace the two statements

```
    cursor.execute("INSERT INTO tblTemps VALUES (?,?,?)", myRec)
    conn.commit()
```

with

```
    try:
        cursor.execute("INSERT INTO tblTemps VALUES (?,?,?)", myRec)
        conn.commit()
    except:
        print ("\nA record for this city already exists")
```

This works as follows:

- first, an attempt is made to execute the statements between `try` and `except`

- if no exception occurs, the `except` clause is skipped and execution of the `try` statement is finished

- if an exception occurs, the `except` clause is executed instead of the `try` clause

Deleting a record

In Example 9, the main program calls a function to delete a record, passing it the name of the database.

There is no need to use the `try ... except` clause here because the program will not crash if you enter the name of a city that does not exist.

The function deletes the record if it is present and then prints the contents of the database – this is useful for testing but could be deleted from a finished application.

Using a `with` statement

Example 9 introduces the `with conn:` statement. Using this statement, any change to the database is automatically committed so you do not need to include the `conn.commit()` statement. However, it will not do any harm if you do include it.

Example 9

The following program deletes a record from `tblTemps`.

```
#Program name: Ch 11 Example 9 deleting a record.py
import sqlite3
def deleteRec(dbname):
    conn = sqlite3.connect (dbname)
    with conn:
        cursor = conn.cursor()
        myCity = input("Enter name of city to delete: ")
        keyfield = "'" + myCity + "'"
        cursor.execute("DELETE FROM tblTemps WHERE city =" +
        keyfield)
        #conn.commit()

    for row in cursor.execute("SELECT * FROM tblTemps"):
        print(row)

#main
deleteRec("cityTemperatures.db")

#keeps the console window open
input ("\nPress Enter to exit")
```

Note: If the `myCity` value is not in the table, no error is indicated when an attempt is made to delete the record.

Updating the database

The SQL command to update the temperature in a given city, for example London, from its current value of 7°C to 10°C is:

```
UPDATE tblTemps
SET temperature = 10
WHERE city = "London"
```

However, in a Python program you will probably want to allow the user to enter the field to be used in the search condition, and the value to which it is to be set. In that case, you need to replace the literal values specified above with string variables containing the data entered by the user. This is shown in the following example.

11

Example 10

Write a program to ask the user which field in the table they wish to amend, and what the new value is to be. Update the record accordingly.

```
#Program name: Ch 11 Example 10 amend CityTemperatures record.py
import sqlite3

def amend():
#print the records before amendment
    with sqlite3.connect("CityTemperatures.db") as conn:
        cursor = conn.cursor()
        for row in cursor.execute("SELECT * FROM tblTemps"):
            print (row)

        keyfield = input("Enter city name of the record to amend: ")
#Put quote marks around city name, e.g. 'London'
        keyfield = "'" + keyfield + "'"

        field = input("Change which field \
        (temperature or localTime)? ")
        newvalue = input("Enter the new value for this field: ")

#Validate the entry - temperature should be numeric or
#program will crash
        try:
            cursor.execute("UPDATE tblTemps SET " + field + "=" +
            newvalue + " WHERE city = " + keyfield)
            print("\nRecord updated")
        except:
            print("\nNo record updated - invalid data entered")

        for row in cursor.execute("SELECT * FROM tblTemps"):
            print (row)
#main
amend()
```

Note: If the data input for `keyField` *or* `field` *does not exist, no error is reported and no change is made to the data.*

Exercises

Use the **Films.db** database for these exercises.

1. Write a program to print all the records in **Films.db**.

2. Write a program to do the following:

   Display a menu of options

   ```
   1. Add a record
   2. Delete a record
   3. Amend a record
   4. Print all records
   5. Exit
   ```

   Implement each of these options as a function.

3. Write a program to do the following:

   Display a menu of options

   ```
   1. Print details of all films
   2. Print all films of a particular genre
   3. Print Film titles, ratings and genre sequenced by genre
      and rating
   4. Print details of all films released in 2016, sequenced
      by title
   5. Exit
   ```

   Implement each of these options as a function.

11

Chapter 12
Introduction to Tkinter

Objectives

- Use Tkinter to create a simple graphical user interface
- Create a window with buttons and label widgets
- Set the size and colour of a window
- Learn how to use the Pack and Grid Geometry Managers to place widgets in a window

The Python Tkinter module

12

First came **Tk**, an open source toolkit which provides a library of interactive **widgets** or **Graphical User Interface (GUI)** elements such as windows, labels, buttons, menus and text entry fields.

Tkinter is a standard Python module providing an interface to the Tk toolkit.

You can use the interactive window to test that it is installed and running correctly.

Load Python's IDLE and import the Tkinter package by typing (all in lowercase):

```
>>> import tkinter
```

Then type

```
>>> import _tkinter
```

This will import the compiled binary associated with the Tkinter package.

Run the test routine by typing:

```
>>> tkinter._test()
```

Press **Enter** and you should see a window like this one:

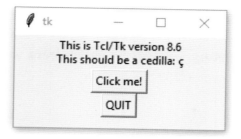

You can click and drag the edges to resize the window, and drag the window around the screen.

Click on the "Click me!" button and you will see square brackets appear around the words.

Close the window by clicking the "QUIT" button. If all this runs correctly you are ready to start!

The "Hello World" program

Example 1

Open a new file in IDLE or use your usual text editor to type the following program.

```
#Program name: Ch 12 Example 1 Hello World
from  tkinter import *
root = Tk()
root.title("Greeting")
Label(root, text = "Hello World").pack()
root.mainloop()
```

Save and run the program. You should see a window like this:

This is a brief description of what each line of the program does.

- The first line after the comment imports all the functions and variables from the Tkinter package, along with their names, so that they can be called directly by these names.

- The second line causes a TK constructor method to create a new top level widget, the main window, and assign it to the variable name `root`.

- The third line sets the title of the window. (The window needs to be enlarged to see the title. Try resizing the window.)

- The fourth line creates a label with the text `Hello World` as a child of the root window, and uses the `pack` method to put it on the window.

- The final line runs the `mainloop()` method for the window. The program will continue to run until you close the window.

Widgets

Widgets are the controls, such as buttons and text entry fields, that you use to interface with the program. They can also be used to display information to the user, in the form of a label or graphic.

Adding and editing a button widget

You can try out the basic process of creating and configuring a Tkinter widget in a window by typing commands in the command interface. This way, you can see the effect of each command as soon as you press **Enter**.

```
>>> from tkinter import *
>>> window = Tk() #creates the top level window called window
>>> button = Button(window, text = "Click me")
```

This displays a blank window. The last statement creates a button named `button`, but it is not yet visible because Tkinter doesn't know where to put it. To insert the button into the window, use the `pack()` method.

```
>>> button.pack()
```

As soon as this statement is executed, the button shows up:

You can move or resize the window using the mouse.

Of course, nothing happens when the button is clicked because we have not specified any action.

All widgets have specific properties associated with them, and a button has a text property which can be used to display the text on a button:

```
>>> button["text"]
'Click me'
```

You can change the text on the button by specifying the new text:

```
>>> button["text"] = "Click here"
```

You will see the window change:

Adding a label widget

The following statements will add a **label widget** to the window:

```
>>> instruction = Label(window, text = "Enter your name")
>>> instruction.pack()
```

Note that if you are never going to refer to the label by its variable name `instruction`, you could in this instance combine these two statements into one, and write

```
>>> Label(window, text = "Enter your name").pack()
```

Example 2 on the next page shows how you can also change the text on a label using the `config` method.

Placing widgets in a window

When you create a widget within a window, Tkinter needs to know where to place it. It is the job of the Geometry Manager to control the placement of objects, and there are three different Geometry Managers available.

The Pack Geometry Manager

The **Pack Geometry Manager** is well suited for windows with just a few widgets which can be placed side by side or one under the other. The label `instruction` above was placed with the Pack Geometry Manager.

The Grid Geometry Manager

The **Grid Geometry Manager** divides the window into a grid of rows and columns, and references each cell in the grid using its grid coordinates.

(0,0)	(0,1)	(0,2)
(1,0)	(1,1)	(1,2)
(2,0)	(2,1)	(2,2)

In addition, you can specify whether the widget should be placed on the left (West), right (East), top (North) or bottom (South) of each cell. You can try this in Exercise 2b at the end of the chapter.

The Place Geometry Manager

The **Place Geometry Manager** allows the program to state exactly where each widget should go, using x and y coordinates, with the top left of the window having coordinates (0, 0).

Responding to user input

There is not much point in having a button which doesn't do anything when clicked. The example below shows how to specify what action should be taken when a button is clicked.

Example 2

The sample program opens a window with a label and two buttons:

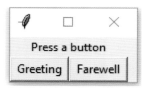

When a button is pressed, the text on the label changes:

 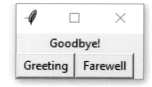

```
#Program name: Ch 12 Example 2 hello goodbye.py
from tkinter import *
window = Tk()

def greeting():
    label.config (text = "Hello!")
def farewell():
    label.config (text = "Goodbye!")

label = Label(window, text = "Press a button")
#columnspan = 2 means that the label will span two columns
label.grid(row = 0, column = 0, columnspan = 2)
button1 = Button(window,text="Greeting",width=7,command=greeting)
button1.grid(row = 1, column = 0)
```

```
button2 = Button(window,text="Farewell",width=7,command=farewell)
button2.grid(row = 1, column = 1)

#run mainloop
window.mainloop()
```

Notes:

- In the definition of button1, the parameter command = greeting tells the program to execute the function greeting() when the button is clicked.

- In this function, the label text is changed using the method config() and specifying the new text to be displayed.

- When button2 is clicked, the function farewell() will be executed.

- window.mainloop() causes the program to run continuously until the window is closed.

Setting window parameters

You can set the size and colour of the window and specify whether it should be resizable. You can also put some "padding" around the button and label widgets, using the parameters padx, pady.

Example 3

Amend the code for Example 2, adding the extra lines as shown below:

```
#Program name: Ch 12 Example 3 hello goodbye.py
#Program places label and two buttons in a window
#Pressing a button changes the label text
#In this version the window parameters are set
from tkinter import *

def greeting():
    label.config (text = "Hello!")

def farewell():
    label.config (text = "Goodbye!")

window = Tk()
window.geometry("200x150")
window.title("Demo")

#Window is not resizable in either direction
window.resizable (False, False)
window.configure(background = "Light blue")
```

```
#Define and place labels and buttons
label = Label(window, text = "Press a button")
label.grid(row = 0,column = 0,columnspan = 2,padx = 20,pady = 20)
button1 = Button(window,text="Greeting",width=7,command=greeting)
button1.grid(row = 1, column = 0, padx = 20)
button2 = Button(window,text="Farewell",width=7,command=farewell)
button2.grid(row = 1, column = 1, padx = 20)

#run mainloop
window.mainloop()
```

The window will now appear like this:

Exercises

1. Write a program to place a button saying "Click here" in a window. When the button is clicked, a message "Hi there!" appears under the button. Give the window a title "Placing a button".

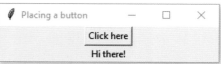

2. (a) Write a program to display, in a light green window size 200 x 120, two buttons saying "Left" and "Right". Under the buttons, display a label saying "left" when the "left" button is pressed, or "right" when the "right" button is pressed. Use the grid manager and padding to place the widgets neatly spaced in the window.

    (b) Left or right justify the labels as appropriate. You will need two functions similar to the following:

```
def leftJustify():
    label.config (text = "left")
    label.grid(row = 1, column = 0, columnspan = 2,
               padx = 30, pady = 10, sticky = W)
```

Chapter 13

Developing an application using Tkinter

Objectives

- Design and implement a data entry form for a given application
- Implement actions to be performed when a button is clicked
- Use a message window to give information to the user
- Close the Tk window and continue or end the program

Sample Application 1

This chapter describes how you might set about developing a GUI application using Tkinter. The sample application will display a data entry screen to enable a teacher or administrator to enter a user ID, first name and surname for a student.

Designing the data input window

You should start by hand drawing a rough design for your form, perhaps something like the image below.

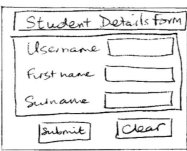

Using frames

In the hand-drawn design above, the form has been divided into three distinct areas – the heading, the input boxes and the buttons. The diagram shows that the top two areas are each to be held in their own **frame**. The buttons will not be in a frame; they will be in the main window.

Using frames is useful because it means that moving anything in one frame will not affect the placement of anything outside the frame. You can also choose to make the background colour of the frames different from the window.

Building the form

The first thing to do is to make a list of all the widgets that are needed, their parent/child relationships, and where they will be placed in the window.

The master window is commonly given the name `root`.

The design shows just two frames, which will each be children of the master window.

The top frame contains one child, namely the form heading.

The second frame contains three text labels and three input fields (entry widgets).

The two buttons are not in a frame, so they are children of the master window.

The list of widgets to be created is as follows:

Widget name	Widget type	Parent	Description
root	Tk	(none)	Main window
frame_heading	Frame	root	Frame around the form heading
(none)	Label	frame_heading	Form heading
frame_entry	Frame	root	Frame around the text labels and input fields
(none)	Label	frame_entry	Label "Username"
(none)	Label	frame_entry	Label "First name"
(none)	Label	frame_entry	Label "Surname"
username	Entry	frame_entry	Data entry box
firstname	Entry	frame_entry	Data entry box
surname	Entry	frame_entry	Data entry box
submit_button	Button	root	Button to submit data
clear_button	Button	root	Button to clear entry boxes

In general, as you never need to change or move labels once they are placed, there is no need to name them.

When data for a student has been entered, the user will submit it by pressing a **Submit** button. This will cause the data to be printed, and the user can click a **Clear** button to clear the fields ready for the user to enter data for the next person. Once all data has been entered, the user can end the program by closing the window using the **X** icon in the top right corner.

Writing the skeleton code

The program code will follow a similar pattern for most Tkinter programs that you will write, so it is useful to start with a skeleton program which acts as the equivalent of a flowchart. Then you can fill in all the statements under each comment line.

```
#Program name: Ch 13 skeleton program.py
#program to allow entry of user ID, surname and first name
from tkinter import *

# function executed when Submit button is pressed
def submit():

# function executed when Clear button is pressed
def clear():

#create a fixed size window
root = Tk()

#place a frame to contain the form heading

#place a frame to contain labels and user entries

#place the form heading

#place the labels

#place the text entry fields

#place the Submit and Clear buttons

#run mainloop to draw the window and start the program running
root.mainloop()
```

Note: By convention, the main or root window in a Tkinter application is named root.

13

Creating the root window

The parameters of the root window will be set in the same way as in Example 3 of the previous chapter.

```
#create a fixed size window
root = Tk()
root.geometry("270x240")
root.title("Student details")
root.resizable (False, False)
root.configure(background = "Light blue")
```

Creating the frames

It's useful to draw a grid over the window design so we can easily see in which row and column within a particular frame each widget is to be placed.

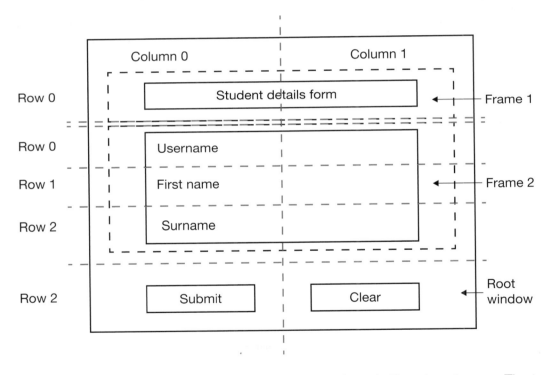

Within each frame, the first row is Row 0, the second row is Row 1 and so on. The two buttons are in the main window, not in a frame, so they are in Row 2 with reference to the window, since Frame 1 is in Row 0 of the window and Frame 2 is in Row 1 of the window. Note that the rows do not have to be the same height – their height is determined by their contents.

The code to place the frames is given below:

```
#place a frame to contain the form heading
frame_heading = Frame(root)
frame_heading.grid(row=0, column=0, columnspan=2, padx=30,
                   pady=5)

#place a frame to contain labels and user entries
frame_entry = Frame(root)
frame_entry.grid(row=1, column=0, columnspan=2, padx=25,
                 pady=10)
```

Notes:

- The heading spans two columns, so the parameter `columnspan=2` is included in the statements which call the `grid()` method.

- We don't want the heading frame to be placed in the top left hand corner of the window. The parameters `padx` and `pady` cause "padding" of the specified number of characters to be included to the left of and above the frame.

Placing the form heading and the labels

The Label widgets are placed next. Notice that as there will be no need to refer to the labels, we do not need to assign them variable names. The grid statement can be included in the definition of the Label widget. (It would not matter if you did give the Label widgets their own names, but it is not necessary to do so.)

```
#place the form heading
Label(frame_heading,text="Student details form",
font=('Arial',16))\
              .grid(row=0, column=0, padx=0, pady=5)

#place the labels
Label(frame_entry, text = "Username: ")\
              .grid(row=0, column=0, padx=10, pady=5)
Label(frame_entry, text = "First name: ")\
              .grid(row=1, column=0, padx=10, pady=10)
Label(frame_entry, text ="Surname: ") \
              .grid(row=2, column=0, padx=10, pady=10)
```

Notes:

- You can specify the size and font style, as well as other optional parameters.
- The \ character indicates that the statement continues on the next line.

Placing the text entry fields

The Entry widget is used for creating a box for the user to enter text. The width is given as 15 characters in the statements below, and the background colour is specified as white.

```
#place the text entry fields
username = Entry(frame_entry, width = 15, bg = "white")
username.grid(row=0, column=1, padx=5,pady=5)

firstname = Entry(frame_entry, width = 15, bg = "white")
firstname.grid(row=1, column=1, padx=5, pady=5)

surname = Entry(frame_entry, width = 15, bg = "white")
surname.grid(row=2, column=1, padx=5, pady=5)
```

Placing the buttons

The **Submit** and **Clear** buttons are created and placed using the Button widget. The parameter `root` indicates that these are placed directly in the window named `root`. The parameter `command = submit` specifies the name of the function to be called when the **Submit** button is pressed.

```
#place the Submit and Clear buttons
submit_button = Button(root, text="Submit",width=7,
                       command=submit)
submit_button.grid(row=2, column=0, padx=0, pady=5)

clear_button = Button(root, text= "Clear", width=7,
                      command=clear)
clear_button.grid(row=2, column=1, padx=0, pady=5)
```

The Submit and Clear functions

These must be placed above the point where the functions are called, so in this example they are placed at the beginning of the program.

The `submit()` function gets the user input from the entry box and prints it. In a more realistic application, these fields could be written to a file or database for later retrieval.

The `clear()` function deletes all the characters input, from character 0 to the last character, signified by END. It then sets the focus to the first input field ready for the next username to be entered.

```
# functions executed when a button is pressed
def submit():
    print("Username",username.get())
    print("First name",firstname.get())
    print("Surname",surname.get())

def clear():
    username.delete(0,END)
    firstname.delete(0,END)
    surname.delete(0,END)
    username.focus_set()
```

Finally, the last statement in the program keeps the window open until you close it in the normal way with the X symbol in the top right hand corner. This will end the program.

```
#run mainloop to draw the window and start the program running
root.mainloop()
```

The final input form

The final input form looks like this:

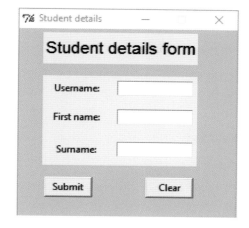

The complete program `Ch 13 Sample app 1 student details form.py` can be downloaded from the program folder on the website www.pgonline.co.uk.

Sample Application 2

In this application, the user will log on by typing a username and password. If the password is incorrect, an error message will be displayed, the username field and the password will be cleared and the user can press a **Password hint** button to help them get their password correct. In this example, the password is "aaaaaa". The user name is not checked. The input screen looks like this:

Once the password has been entered correctly, another message window is displayed inviting the user to continue. Once they press **OK**, the message box and the main window close and control passes back to the program, where the user could enter some data, play a game, take a test or perform any other task. In this example the program simply prints "carry on now…" and ends.

The password typed by the user will be replaced by asterisks on the screen, as a security measure. This is achieved by including the parameter `show = "*"` in the Entry widget:

```
entry_password = Entry(frame_entry,width=15,bg="white",show = "*")
```

Using a message box

The messagebox widget is not one of Tkinter's standard widgets, so you need to include the statement `from tkinter import messagebox` at the top of the program.

A message box is useful for alerting the user to an error or to give them information. In this application we will use two message boxes. The first one pops up with a message when they press a **Password hint** button if they have forgotten their password. It is common practice in many login routines to include a button to click if you have forgotten your password – normally the system will reset the password and email you a new one.

The Python code to display the message box is

```
messagebox.showinfo(title = "Password hint",
                    message = "Hint: Try password aaaaaa")
```

This generates the pop-up window, and the user must click OK to continue.

Once the user presses the **Submit** button, the program checks the password and if correct, displays a message "Password accepted" and a message box to allow the user to continue.

Note: The password and hint in this example are clearly used for testing purposes only; in a real situation, the password and the hint would be something that the user had originally supplied, such as a hint "Grandmother's birthday" to accompany a password such as GMa221155, to remind them what password they had specified.

Closing the Tkinter GUI

The window named `root` is closed in the `submit` function with the statement

```
root.destroy()
```

Control then passes back to the statement following the `root.mainloop()` statement and the program continues.

The complete listing is shown below.

```
#Program name: Ch 13 Sample app 2 validate password aaaaaa.py
#Program asks user to login, then checks password
#In this program, password is "aaaaaa"

from tkinter import *
from tkinter import messagebox

def submit():
    password = entry_password.get()
    username = entry_username.get()
    messageAlert = Label(root,width = 30)
    messageAlert.grid(row=3, column=0, columnspan=2, padx=5,
    pady=5)
```

```
    if password != "aaaaaa":
        messageAlert.config(text = "Password incorrect")
        entry_username.delete(0,"END")
        entry_password.delete(0,"END")
        entry_username.focus_set()

    else:
        messageAlert.config(text = "Password accepted")
        print("password accepted")
        print("Username: ", username)
        print("Password: ", password)
        messagebox.showinfo(title = "Password OK",
        message = "Press OK to continue")
        root.destroy()

# display a message box with a hint for password
def hint():
    messagebox.showinfo(title = "Password hint",
                        message = "Hint: Try password aaaaaa")

#create the main window
root = Tk()
root.geometry("250x180")
root.title("Login Screen")
root.resizable (False, False)
root.configure(background = "Light blue")

#place a frame round labels and user entries
frame_entry = Frame(root)
#frame_entry.pack(padx = 10, pady = 10)
frame_entry.grid(row=0, column=0, columnspan = 2,
                 padx = 10, pady = 10)

#place a frame around the buttons
frame_buttons = Frame(root)
frame_buttons.grid(row = 2, column = 0, columnspan = 3,
                   padx = 10, pady = 10)

#place the labels and text entry fields
Label(frame_entry, text = "Enter username: ").grid(row = 0,
      column = 0, padx = 5, pady = 5)
```

```
entry_username = Entry(frame_entry, width = 15, bg = "white")
entry_username.grid(row = 0, column = 1, padx = 5, pady = 5)

Label(frame_entry, text = "Enter password: ").grid(row = 1,
        column = 0, padx = 10, pady = 10)

# The parameter show = "*" will cause asterisks to appear
# instead of the characters typed by the user
entry_password = Entry(frame_entry, width=15, bg = "white",
                        show = "*")
entry_password.grid(row = 1, column = 1, padx = 5,pady = 5)

#place the submit button
submit_button = Button(frame_buttons, text = "Submit",
                        width = 8, command = submit)
submit_button.grid(row = 0, column = 0, padx = 5, pady = 5)

#place the Hint button
hint_button = Button(frame_buttons, text = "Password hint",
                        width = 15, command = hint)
hint_button.grid(row = 0, column = 1, padx = 5, pady = 5)

#run mainloop
root.mainloop()
print("carry on now...")
```

13

Sample Application 3

This application allows a user (for example, a teacher) to create a multiple choice test consisting of several questions which could be saved in a text file or database. The input window will look like this:

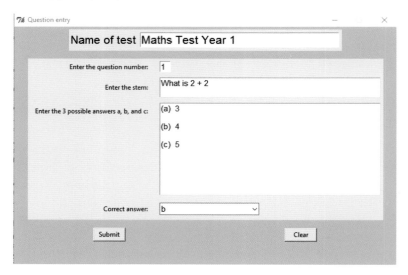

The skeleton code is given below. There are several new features covered in the code. Notes below the code explain the lines indicated by *Note 1*, *Note 2* etc.

```
#Program name: Ch13 Sample app 3 multiple choice test entry.py
#Program to allow entry of questions for a multiple choice test
#Questions and correct answer are printed
#and could be sent to a file for permanent storage
from tkinter import *
from tkinter import ttk                                          Note 1


# functions executed when a button is pressed
def submit():
    if questionNumber.get() == "1":
        print("Test name", testname.get())
    print("Question number: ",questionNumber.get())
    print("Question stem: ",questionStem.get(1.0,END))           Note 2
    print("Possible answers: ")
    print(possibleAnswers.get(1.0, END))
    print("Correct answer: ", correctAnswer.get(), "\n")
```

13

```
def clear():
    questionNumber.delete(0,END)
    questionStem.delete(1.0,END)
    possibleAnswers.delete(1.0,END)
    correctAnswer.delete(0,END)
    questionNumber.focus_set()

#create a fixed size window
root = Tk()
root.geometry("700x450")
root.title("Question entry")
root.resizable (False, False)
root.configure(background = "Light blue")

#place a frame to contain the form heading
frame_heading = Frame(root)
frame_heading.grid(row = 0, column = 0, columnspan = 2,
                   padx =3 0, pady = 5)

#place a frame to contain labels and user entries
frame_entry = Frame(root)
frame_entry.grid(row = 1, column = 0, columnspan = 2,
                 padx = 25, pady = 10)

#place the form heading
Label(frame_heading, text = "Name of test", font = ('Arial',
16)).grid(row = 0, column = 0, padx = 0, pady = 5)

#place the labels
Label(frame_entry, text = "Enter the question number: ")\
      .grid(row=0, column=0, padx=10, pady=5, sticky=E)
Label(frame_entry, text = "Enter the stem: ")\
      .grid(row=1, column=0, padx=10, pady=5, sticky=E)
Label(frame_entry,
      text = "Enter the 3 possible answers a, b, and c: ")\
      .grid(row=2, column=0, padx=10, pady=10)
Label(frame_entry, text ="Correct answer: ") \
      .grid(row=3,column=0,padx=10,pady=10)
```

Note 3

13

```
#place the text entry fields
testname= Entry(frame_heading, width=30, font=('Arial', 16))
testname.grid(row=0, column=1, padx=5, pady=5)

questionNumber = Entry(frame_entry, width=2, font=('Arial', 11))
questionNumber.grid(row=0, column=1, padx=5, pady=5, sticky=W)

questionStem = Text(frame_entry, width=50, height=2,
                    bg="white", font=('Arial', 11))
questionStem.grid(row=1, column=1, padx=5, pady=5)

possibleAnswers = Text(frame_entry, width=50, height=10,
                       bg="white", font=('Arial', 11))
possibleAnswers.grid(row=2, column=1, padx=5, pady=5)

#Import ttk at the top of the program to use Combobox
correctAnswer = ttk.Combobox(frame_entry, text="a",
                             font=('Arial', 11))

correctAnswer.grid(row=3, column=1, padx=5, pady=5, sticky=W)
correctAnswer.config(values=("a","b","c"))

#place the Submit and Clear buttons
submit_button = Button(root, text="Submit", width=7,
command = submit)
submit_button.grid(row=2, column=0, padx=0, pady=5)
clear_button = Button(root,text="Clear", width=7, command=clear)
clear_button.grid(row=2, column=1, padx=0, pady=5)

#Here is where you would open a file
#ready to store the test questions and answers
print("Open the file math1.txt")

#run mainloop to draw the window and start the program running
root.mainloop()
print("carry on...")
```

Note 4

Note 5

Note 6

Note 7

Notes

Note 1:   The combo box, which is used here to display the three options a, b, c for the correct answer and allow the user to select one of these options, is not a standard widget in Tkinter. It needs to be imported from the module ttk, which contains additional widgets.

Note 2:   `1.0` refers to the position at the start of the text box, and `END` refers to the position after the last character. The statement:

```
questionStem.get(1.0,END)
```

will get all the characters in the question stem. We could, as an alternative way of coding, assign the stem to a variable `stem` and print `stem`.

Note 3:   We can specify whether the text should be left- or right-justified, or hugging the top or bottom of an entry box, by specifying W for West (left-justified), E for East (right-justified), NE for top right, etc.

Note 4:   We are using Text widgets to enter both the question stem and the possible answers for the multiple choice question, because the text will span several lines. The height and width of the text box is specified – we've allowed up to 2 rows for the question stem and up to 10 rows for the possible answers.

Note 5:   This is where you need to specify that `Combobox` is a ttk widget.

Note 6:   In this program the questions entered are not stored in a file, they are just printed. Normally you would write them to a file so that the test could be read at a later date by someone sitting the test.

Note 7:   You must call `mainloop()` once and only once in a program. Once you close the main window by clicking the **X** icon in the top right corner or calling `root.destroy()`, control passes to the next statement in the program. The Tk application and widgets are destroyed, and you cannot run `mainloop()` a second time to reopen the window.

Exercises

1. Amend Sample Application 1 so that the program stores student details in a text file or creates a database file.

2. Write a program to retrieve and print the details for a student with a username entered by the user.

3. Write a program which allows a user to choose a username and password. The password must be at least 6 characters, in which case a message "password accepted" is displayed. Otherwise, a message "Password must be at least 6 characters" is displayed and the fields are cleared for the user to re-enter their username and password.

4. Amend the program in Sample Application 3 to store the test in a text file instead of printing the questions. Test your program by entering at least 3 questions.

Chapter 14
Program design

Objectives

- To identify the major tasks to be performed in a solution to a given problem
- To plan the structure of the program
- To split the program into a number of self-contained functions

Planning a program

As the requirements of a system become more complex, it becomes essential to plan out a solution on paper before starting to write code. There are various "tools" you can use to help with this, including

- structure diagrams
- pseudocode
- flowcharts

In this chapter we will look at a sample task and plan a solution by breaking the problem down into its component parts or subtasks, and then writing modules (functions) for each subtask.

The sample task

In Sample Application 3 in Chapter 13 we looked at how to write a program to allow a teacher to enter questions for a multiple choice test. We will expand the problem in this chapter to start by presenting a menu of options to the teacher, to allow them to create a new test, add to an existing test, print the contents of a test file or edit a particular question. The test will be stored in a text file.

Step 1 – Identify the major tasks

We can identify several tasks that need to be performed in the program. Start by writing a list, and then look at how the program can be split up into different self-contained functions, with a main program which calls the functions. A first attempt might look like this:

```
Display the menu
Get the user choice and validate it
Create a new file and add questions
Append questions to an existing file
Edit an existing question
Print contents of file
```

Step 2 – Add a structure to incorporate these functions

Many programs will have a number of different options from which the user can choose. This is usually achieved by displaying a menu and asking the user to choose an option, which is then validated. We can visualise that the menu would look something like this:

```
Option 1: Create a new test file
Option 2: Add questions to an existing test
Option 3: Edit questions in an existing test
Option 4: Print the contents of a test file
Option 5: Quit
Please enter your choice:
```

The program will display the menu, get the user choice, validate it, and carry out the chosen option.

We can express this structure in **pseudocode**, which uses statements and structures similar to those that you may use in Python, but without paying attention to the syntax of a particular language. A possible outline structure is shown below:

```
choice = None
display menu
call function getMenuChoice to get and validate choice
if choice = "1"
   call function to create new file
else if choice = "2"
   call function to open existing file
   call function to accept user input and write to file
else if choice = "3"
   call function to edit question and write to file
```

14

```
else if choice = "4"
    call function to print the file
endif
if file has been opened
    close the file
endif
print goodbye message
```

Step 3 – Add more detail where required

Next you need to decide whether the program should use a GUI or a text interface. Once you have made a decision, you can either use pseudocode to plan the logic, or it may be easier just to start coding.

To code the program, you could first create the main program, which displays the menu, calls a function to get and validate the choice, and then calls a different function depending on the choice. For each of these functions, write a "stub"; e.g. the function heading and a print statement – for example,

```
def editQuestions():
    print("Option 3 Edit questions chosen")
```

This will demonstrate that the function has been called at the correct point in the logic, and the processing can be added later on.

Get that working correctly, and then code each function in turn.

14

Exercises

1. (a) Design a structured program which displays a menu of shapes. The user then inputs the name of a shape, which could be either "circle" or "rectangle", together with either the radius or the length of each side. The program calculates its area and prints it.

   (b) Write the program as a series of functions. *(Use the formula $\pi \times radius^2$ for the area of a circle, and length x width for a rectangle.)*

2. Code the program for the sample task described in this chapter. Do not code the functions for Options 3 and 4. Instead, write "stubs" so that the whole program can be tested.

Chapter 15
Testing and debugging

Objectives

- Write a test plan for a program
- Test a program to detect syntax and logic errors
- Use the Python debugging module pdb

Drawing up a test plan

For all your programs, you need to draw up a test plan to make sure that the program will run correctly whatever the user enters. Every program that you write is likely to contain some syntax errors the first time you run it, but once you have corrected these, you need to ensure that no logic errors remain.

In this chapter you will practise debugging a program with the aid of Python's debugging module, pdb.

Example 1

This program was given as an exercise in Chapter 6. The specification is as follows:

A Dramatic Society wants to record the number of tickets sold for each of their four performances. Ask the user to enter the number of tickets sold for each performance. The number must be between 0 and 120. Print an error message if an invalid number is entered, and ask them to re-enter until they enter a valid number. Print the total number of tickets sold and the average attendance for a performance.

The first task is to write a test plan. You need to test both valid and invalid entries.

- It is possible the user may accidentally type a non-numeric character. What would happen in this case?

- Test data should always include the boundary values (0 and 120 in this case), since entering data at the boundaries of legitimate ranges is a common source of logic errors.
- Calculate what the expected results are for valid test data.

Here is a test plan.

No.	Test purpose	Test data	Expected outcome	Actual outcome
1.	Test user input of non-numeric character	Enter choice = "asd"	Invalid choice – user asked to re-enter	
2.	Test data outside valid range for first performance	Performance 1=200 Then enter 40,80,100,90 (typical data)	Invalid data – user asked to re-enter Total = 310 Average = 77.5	
3.	Test boundary values	0, 120, 80, 40	Total = 240, Average = 60	
4.	Test data just outside boundary	-1,121,80,40 Then enter 0,120,80,40	Invalid data – user asked to re-enter after -1 and 121 entered. Total = 240, Average = 60	
5.	Test a correct entry for performance 1 followed by an incorrect entry for performance 2	Performance 1=100 Then enter 200, (not accepted), 30,40,50	Total 220, Average = 55	

The version of the program shown below has logic errors in it.

```
#Program name: Ch 15 Example 1 with errors.py
#Validates and counts tickets sold over 4 performances

total = 0

for performance in range(5):
    flag = False
        number = input("Please enter tickets sold for performance"
                + str(performance+1) + ": ")
```

```
   while flag == False:
      try:
         int(number)
      except ValueError:
         print ("This is not a valid number")
         flag = False
      else:
         flag = True
      if flag:
         number = int(number)
         if number in range (120):
            total += number
         else:
            number = input
            ("Please re-enter tickets sold for performance: "
            + str(performance+1) + ": ")

average = total/4
print("\nTotal tickets sold: ",total)
print("\nAverage number of tickets per performance ", average)
input("\nPress Enter to exit ")
```

The output from Test 1 is:

```
Please enter tickets sold for performance 1: asd
This is not a valid number
This is not a valid number
This is not a valid number
This is not a valid number … (continuous loop)
```

You can terminate the program by selecting *Shell, Interrupt Execution* from the menu in the Python Shell window, or by pressing the shortcut key combination **Ctrl-C**.

> **Q1** Look through the above code carefully. Can you see any logic errors?
> You can load the program (*Ch15 Example 1 with errors.py*) and run it. Try and correct the error, and then try the other tests. You will find that other errors also become apparent.

Python module pdb

Using the commands in this module enables you to trace through each step of a program, and print the values of any variables at any point. It can be a very useful tool for finding an elusive logic error.

Example 2

This mini-tutorial uses a simple program to demonstrate how the debugger works.

1. First of all, you need to import the pdb module at the top of the program.

2. Next, decide where you want the tracing to start.

```
#Program name: Ch 15 Example 2 Using pdb.py
import pdb
x = int(input("Enter first number: "))
y = int(input("Enter second number: "))
pdb.set_trace()
if x == y:
    z = x*x
elif x > y:
    z = x - y
else:
    z = x + y
print("x =", x," y =", y," z =", z)
```

3. Now run the program.

    When your program reaches the set_trace command, it will stop and display the statement that will execute next. The prompt, (Pdb) will be displayed.

    You will see the following output:

    ```
    Enter first number: 10
    Enter second number: 12
    > (pathname) \ch 15 example 2 using pdb.py(6)<module>()
    -> if x == y:
    (Pdb)
    ```

4. Enter the command n (which stands for "Next"). The next command will be executed. You can keep pressing n to trace through the program. Alternatively, having entered n once, you can just press Enter, which repeats the previous debugging command.

5. At any time when the prompt is displayed, you can print the value of any variable. Type p x at the prompt to print the variable x, or p x,y to print both x and y. The output will then look something like:

    ```
    (Pdb) n
    -> elif x > y:
    (Pdb) p x
    10
    (Pdb) p x,y
    (10, 12)
    (Pdb)
    ```

6. To stop tracing and continue running the program, type c for Continue.

7. Alternatively, type q for Quit, which crashes the program and exits.

Exercises

1. The following program was set as an exercise in Chapter 6.

Write a program to ask a user to enter a new password. The password must be between 8 and 15 characters long and have at least one lowercase letter, one uppercase letter and one numeric character. If it does not, the user should repeatedly be asked to enter a different password until they enter a valid one.

```python
#Program name: Ch 15 Exercise 1 with errors.py
#validates a new password
ucaseLetters = ["A","B","C","D","E","F","G","H","I",\
                "J","K","L","M","N","O","P","Q","R",\
                "S","T","U","V","W","X","Y","Z"]
#define the lowercase letters
lcaseLetters=[]
for letter in ucaseLetters:
    lcaseLetter = letter.lower()
    lcaseLetters.append(lcaseLetter)
numbers = ["0","1","2","3","4","5","6","7","8","9"]
print ("""Your password must contain at least
        one uppercase letter
        one lowercase letter
        and one number.
        It must be between 8 and 15 characters long\n""")
#input password
passwordChecks = 0
password = input("Please enter new password: ")
while passwordChecks < 3:
    if len(password)>=8 and len(password)<=15:
        passwordChecks += 1
        for letter in password:
            if letter in lcaseLetters:
                passwordChecks += 1
            if letter in ucaseLetters:
                passwordChecks += 1
    if passwordChecks < 3:
        password = input("\nInvalid password - please re-enter: ")
        passwordChecks = 0
print("\nPassword accepted")
```

(a) Write a test plan to thoroughly test the finished program.

(b) James has written the code above, but it does not work always work correctly. Type the code, or download it from the website pgonline.co.uk. (It is named *Ch 15 Exercise 1 with errors.py*.) Run the tests in your test plan and fill in the actual results.

(c) Debug the program. You could use the pdb module to help do this.

2. The following program was set as an exercise in Chapter 6. It holds an encrypted password. When the user types their password, it compares it with the stored encrypted one and if the two do not match, the user is asked to enter another password.

```python
#Program name: Ch 15 Exercise 2 with errors.py
storedPassword = "EHQAB6"
passwordOK = False
password = input("Please enter your password: ")
while not passwordOK:
    codedPassword = ""
    for num in range(len(password)):
        asciiValue = ord(password[num])
        codedValue = asciiValue + 3
        if codedValue > ord("X"):
            codedValue -= 26
        codedPassword = codedPassword + chr(codedValue)
    if storedPassword == codedPassword:
        print("Password accepted")
        passwordOK = True
    else:
        input("Password incorrect - please re-enter: ")
```

(a) Write a test plan to thoroughly test the finished program.

(b) Nadia has written the above code, but it does not always work correctly. Type the code, or download it from the website pgonline.co.uk. (It is named *Ch 15 Exercise 2 with errors.py*.) Run the tests in your test plan and fill in the actual results.

(c) Debug the program. You could use the pdb module to help do this.

You've reached the end … congratulations!

15

I